The Occasional Speeches of Justice Oliver Wendell Holmes

The Occasional Speeches of Justice Oliver Wendell Holmes

Compiled by Mark DeWolfe Howe

THE BELKNAP PRESS
OF HARVARD UNIVERSITY PRESS
Cambridge, Massachusetts
1962

Printed in the United States of America
Distributed in Great Britain by Oxford University Press, London
Library of Congress Catalog Card Number: 62-13267

Contents

Contents

Contents

Contents

Foreword

BETWEEN 1891 and 1913 Justice Holmes assembled and published "chance utterances of faith and doubt . . . for a few friends who will care to keep them." The five separate editions of the *Speeches* are now out of print and it seemed advisable to the President and Fellows of Harvard College, in whom the copyright is now vested, that the speeches published in the last edition should be made available to a larger circle than that for which Holmes first published the collection. That decision led to another—to add to the contents of the 1913 edition of the *Speeches* all the occasional addresses of the Justice's which survive in authentic versions. This compilation is the result of that decision. It should be noted that the source of the published text is indicated in the case of each address not included in the last printing of the *Speeches* (Little, Brown, and Company, 1934). Where no source is indicated the text is taken from that volume.

Those who are familiar with the writings of Justice Holmes will immediately notice that a few of his most important addresses are omitted from this collection. Such papers as "The Path of the Law" and "Law in Science—Science in Law" evidently seemed to Holmes to be something more significant than "chance utterances of faith and doubt," for they were excluded from each edition of the *Speeches*. They are not, in other words, "occasional" addresses and did not seem to be fitting parts of this particular whole. They are, furthermore, readily available in the volume of *Collected Legal Papers* and in other compilations of Holmes's writings. The more questionable decision, perhaps, was to include in this collection speeches which Holmes himself had not seen fit to publish in any compilation. Very clearly some of the occasions and the remarks celebrating them were of such trivial importance and parochial significance that Holmes's judgment to let them pass into oblivion, even among his friends, was natural and appropriate. Yet it seems that, for a generation which has interest in the shape of the speaker's mind and in the structure of his faith and doubt, it is important that the surviving record of this special form of his expression should be published in its entirety. One of the prices which a man pays for his greatness is that his every word, spoken in public, becomes a matter of legitimate public interest.

It should be added, perhaps, that two speeches, surviving in manuscript, are omitted from this collection. The one was a brief address to the Twentieth Regiment, Massachusetts Volunteers, delivered on December 10, 1892. It is omitted since its most significant passages were incorporated almost verbatim in "The Soldier's Faith." The other, a response to the Norfolk Bar's memorial to Asaph Churchill, though prepared for exercises scheduled for February 21, 1898, was never delivered because the ceremony was postponed. Furthermore, the most effective passage in the response was later used by Holmes in his memorial to Arthur P. Bonney and Governor Greenhalge.

Some readers may regret the decision not to supplement the speeches with explanatory annotation. The principal reason for not doing so is that this volume is conceived primarily to be a new edition of the *Speeches*, a volume which was not dressed in the attire of scholarship. It seemed appropriate, however, with respect to a few of the speeches not published in earlier editions and honoring men whose names are not now generally remembered briefly to identify them.

November 1961 M. DeW. H.
Cambridge, Massachusetts

REMARKS AT THE HARVARD COMMENCEMENT DINNER

June 22, 1880

Mr. President: A man who has a retrospect of nearly twenty years since his own Commencement Day is surprised to find that it seems nearer than many later events. Memory spreads a floor of light from summit to summit of our experience, across which our vision moves easily and uninterrupted. Between there lie broad valleys wrapped in darkness, and many men wrapped in sleep. But we see them not. Some of those who later wrote their names upon the tablets of this hall come back to my recollection almost more vividly, as I saw them in our college days, than when our brotherhood was cemented in the ranks of the Twentieth Massachusetts. Henry Abbott, the youngest of seniors, comes before me not less plainly than the captain, marching with careless step and sword dangling from his wrist like a cane, to what seemed certain death; not less plainly than the most brilliant of regimental commanders, who fell at the head of his regiment in the Wilderness—a career of glory already completed at twenty-two. Henry Ropes is no longer the bluff, wise Christian captain who fell at

Source: Harvard Register, 1880 (July 1880), p. 152.

Gettysburg, but the member of the Crew and the president of the Hasty Pudding. Frank Bartlett is a tall young sophomore of striking figure; not that other of our captains who, after he had more than paid his debt of suffering to his country with us, pressed again and again into the field, to suffer and to shine still more—the gallant and gentle soldier whose voice in this place we all remember so well.

Two-thirds of the life of a generation has gone by since then; and when I thus put the past by the side of the present some contrasts begin to appear. The College was metropolitan even in my day. Now it is cosmopolitan. More than physical causes have been at work. In every department of knowledge, what wonderful things have been done to solicit the interest and to stir the hopes of new inquirers! Every thing is interesting when you understand it, when you see its connection with other things, and, in the end, with all other things. And how much of all that has been accomplished to make that possible has been done within the last twenty years! To speak only of my own profession, the law, it is enough to those who are interested in its broader aspects to say that the first book of Sir Henry Maine was published the year I graduated. Since then great contributions have been made; and I think we may affirm with pride, that not the least important of them have come from the great lawyer who presides over our own Law School, Professor Langdell.

It would be bold to say that, with these increased advantages, there has been a corresponding increase in enthusiasm. The Cambridge graduate has always been a little *blasé*, intellectually speaking. Perhaps it is somewhat the fashion to doubt whether life is worth living, to believe that "nothing is new, nothing is true, and it's no matter." But, when it comes to the practical emergencies of life, it seems to me that the graduates of later days have shown that they are of the same stuff as their brothers and their fathers. If not, so much the worse for the brothers and fathers, say I, when I think of the young lawyers, at least, who are coming forward. But in the spiritual emergencies, which are not less real than the practical, I could wish them to remember that the distinction of the scholar is almost our only counterpoise to the distinction of wealth. Where shall chivalrous faith rise above the cynicism of business if not in his person? Life will prove itself worth living if he puts his ambition high enough, if he remembers and believes the noble words of the President of the University—that the duty of the scholar in this country is to make poverty respectable.

MEMORIAL DAY

An Address Delivered May 30, 1884, at Keene, N. H., Before John Sedgwick Post No. 4, Grand Army of the Republic

Not long ago I heard a young man ask why people still kept up Memorial Day, and it set me thinking of the answer. Not the answer that you and I should give to each other—not the expression of those feelings that, so long as you and I live, will make this day sacred to memories of love and grief and heroic youth—but an answer which should command the assent of those who do not share our memories, and in which we of the North and our brethren of the South could join in perfect accord.

So far as this last is concerned, to be sure, there is no trouble. The soldiers who were doing their best to kill one another felt less of personal hostility, I am very certain, than some who were not imperilled by their mutual endeavors. I have heard more than one of those who had been gallant and distinguished officers on the Confederate side say that they had had no such feeling. I know that I and those whom I knew best had not. We believed that it was most desirable that the North should win; we believed in the principle that the Union is indissoluble; we, or many of us at least, also believed that the conflict was inevitable, and that slavery had lasted long enough. But we equally believed that those who stood against us held just as sacred convictions that were the opposite of ours, and we respected them as every man with a heart must respect those who give all for their belief. The experience of battle soon taught its lesson even to those who came into the field more bitterly disposed. You could not stand up day after day in those indecisive contests where overwhelming victory was impossible because neither side would run as they ought when beaten, without getting at last something of the same brotherhood for the enemy that the north pole of a magnet has for the south—each working in an opposite sense to the other, but each unable to get along without the other. As it was then, it is now. The soldiers of the war need no explanations; they can join in commemorating a soldier's death with feelings not different in kind, whether he fell toward them or by their side.

But Memorial Day may and ought to have a meaning also for those who do not share our memories. When men have instinctively agreed to celebrate an anniversary, it will be found that there is some thought or feeling behind it which is too large to be dependent upon associations alone. The Fourth of July, for instance, has still its serious aspect, although we no longer should think of rejoicing like children that we have escaped from an outgrown control, although we have achieved not only our national but our moral independence and know it far too profoundly to make a talk about it, and although an Englishman can join in the celebration without a scruple. For, stripped of the temporary associations which gave rise to it, it is now the moment when by common consent we pause to become conscious of our national life and to rejoice in it, to recall what our country has done for each of us, and to ask ourselves what we can do for our country in return.

So to the indifferent inquirer who asks why Memorial Day is still kept up we may answer, It celebrates and solemnly reaffirms from year to year a national act of enthusiasm and faith. It embodies in the most impressive form our belief that to act with enthusiasm and faith is the condition of acting greatly. To fight out a war, you must believe something and want something with all your might. So must you do to carry anything else to an end worth reaching. More than that, you must be willing to commit yourself to a course, perhaps a long and hard one, without being able to foresee exactly where you will come out. All that is required of you is that you should go somewhither as hard as ever you can. The rest belongs to fate. One may fall—at the beginning of the charge or at the top of the earthworks; but in no other way can he reach the rewards of victory.

When it was felt so deeply as it was on both sides that a man ought to take part in the war unless some conscientious scruple or strong practical reason made it impossible, was that feeling simply the requirement of a local majority that their neighbors should agree with them? I think not: I think the feeling was right—in the South as in the North. I think that, as life is action and passion, it is required of a man that he should share the passion and action of his time at peril of being judged not to have lived.

If this be so, the use of this day is obvious. It is true that I cannot argue a man into a desire. If he says to me, Why should I wish to know the secrets of philosophy? Why seek to decipher the hidden laws of creation that are graven upon the tablets of the rocks, or to unravel the history of civilization that is woven in the tissue of our jurisprudence, or to do any great work, either of speculation or of practical affairs? I cannot answer him; or at least my answer is as little worth making for any effect it will have upon his wishes as if he asked why should I eat this, or drink that. You must begin by wanting to. But although desire cannot be imparted by argument, it can be by contagion. Feeling begets feeling, and great feeling begets great feeling. We can hardly share the emotions that make this day to us the most sacred day of the year, and embody them in ceremonial pomp, without in some degree imparting them to those who come after us. I believe from the bottom of my heart that our memorial halls and statues and tablets, the tattered flags of our regiments gathered in the Statehouses, and this day with its funeral march and decorated graves, are worth more to our young men by way of chastening and inspiration than the monuments of another hundred years of peaceful life could be.

But even if I am wrong, even if those who come after us are to forget all that we hold dear, and the future is to teach and kindle its children in ways as yet unrevealed, it is enough for us that to us this day is dear and sacred.

Accidents may call up the events of the war. You see a battery of guns go by at a trot, and for a moment you are back at White Oak Swamp, or Antietam, or on the Jerusalem Road. You hear a few shots fired in the distance, and for an instant your heart stops as you say to yourself, The skirmishers are at it, and listen for the long roll of fire from the main line. You meet an old comrade after many years of absence; he recalls the moment when you were nearly surrounded by the enemy, and again there comes up to you that swift and cunning thinking on which once hung life or freedom—Shall I stand the best chance if I try the pistol or the sabre on that man who means to stop me? Will he get his carbine free before I reach him, or can I kill him first? These and the thousand other events we have known are called up, I say, by accident, and, apart from accident, they lie forgotten.

But as surely as this day comes round we are in the presence of the dead. For one hour, twice a year at least—at the regimental dinner, where the ghosts sit at table more numerous than the living, and on this day when we decorate their graves—the dead come back and live with us.

I see them now, more than I can number, as once I saw them on this earth. They are the same bright figures, or their counterparts, that come also before your eyes; and when I speak of those who were my brothers, the same words describe yours.

I see a fair-haired lad, a lieutenant, and a captain on whom life had begun somewhat to tell, but still young, sitting by the long mess-table in camp before the regiment left the State, and wondering how many of those who gathered in our tent could hope to see the end of what was then beginning. For neither of them was that destiny reserved. I remember, as I awoke from my first long stupor in the hospital after the battle of Ball's Bluff, I heard the doctor say, "He was a beautiful boy," and I knew that one of those two speakers was no more. The other, after passing harmless through all the previous battles, went into Fredericksburg with strange premonition of the end, and there met his fate.

I see another youthful lieutenant as I saw him in the Seven Days, when I looked down the line at Glendale. The officers were at the head of their companies. The advance was beginning. We caught each other's eye and saluted. When next I looked, he was gone.

I see the brother of the last—the flame of genius and daring in his face—as he rode before us into the wood of Antietam, out of which came only dead and deadly wounded men. So, a little later, he rode to his death at the head of his cavalry in the Valley.

In the portraits of some of those who fell in the civil wars of England, Vandyke has fixed on canvas the type of those who stand before my memory. Young and gracious figures, somewhat remote and proud, but with a melancholy and sweet kindness. There is upon their faces the shadow of approaching fate, and the glory of generous acceptance of it. I may say of them, as I once heard it said of two Frenchmen, relics of the *ancien régime*, "They were very gentle. They cared nothing for their lives." High breeding, romantic chivalry—we who have seen these men can never believe that the power of money or the enervation of pleasure has put an end to them. We know that life may still be lifted into poetry and lit with spiritual charm.

But the men not less, perhaps even more, characteristic of New England, were the Puritans of our day. For the Puritan still lives in New England, thank God! and will live there so long as New England lives and keeps her old renown. New England is not dead yet. She still is mother of a race of conquerors—stern men, little given to the expression of their feelings, sometimes careless of the graces, but fertile, tenacious, and knowing only duty. Each of you, as I do, thinks of a hundred such that he has known. I see one—grandson of a hard rider of the Revolution and bearer of his historic name—who was with us at Fair Oaks, and afterwards for five days and nights in front of the enemy the only sleep that he would take was what he could snatch sitting erect in his uniform and resting his back against a hut. He fell at Gettysburg.

His brother, a surgeon, who rode, as our surgeons so often did, wherever the troops would go, I saw kneeling in ministration to a wounded man just in rear of our line at Antietam, his horse's bridle round his arm—the next moment his ministrations were ended. His senior associate survived all the wounds and perils of the war, but, not yet through with duty as he understood it, fell in helping the helpless poor who were dying of cholera in a Western city.

I see another quiet figure, of virtuous life and silent

ways, not much heard of until our left was turned at Petersburg. He was in command of the regiment as he saw our comrades driven in. He threw back his left wing, and the advancing tide of defeat was shattered against his iron wall. He saved an army corps from disaster, and then a round shot ended all for him.

There is one who on this day is always present to my mind. He entered the army at nineteen, a second lieutenant. In the Wilderness, already at the head of his regiment, he fell, using the moment that was left him of life to give all his little fortune to his soldiers. I saw him in camp, on the march, in action. I crossed debatable land with him when we were rejoining the army together. I observed him in every kind of duty, and never in all the time that I knew him did I see him fail to choose that alternative of conduct which was most disagreeable to himself. He was indeed a Puritan in all his virtues, without the Puritan austerity; for, when duty was at an end, he who had been the master and leader became the chosen companion in every pleasure that a man might honestly enjoy. In action he was sublime. His few surviving companions will never forget the awful spectacle of his advance alone with his company in the streets of Fredericksburg. In less than sixty seconds he would become the focus of a hidden and annihilating fire from a semicircle of houses. His first platoon had vanished under it in an instant, ten men falling dead by his side. He had quietly turned back to where the other half of his company was waiting, had given the order, "Second platoon, forward!" and was again moving on, in obedience to superior command, to certain and useless death, when the order he was obeying was countermanded. The end was distant only a few seconds; but if you had seen him with his indifferent carriage, and sword swinging from his finger like a cane, you never would have suspected that he was doing more than conducting a company drill on the camp parade ground. He was little more than a boy, but the grizzled corps commanders knew and admired him; and for us, who not only admired, but loved, his death seemed to end a portion of our life also.

There is one grave and commanding presence that you all would recognize, for his life has become a part of our common history. Who does not remember the leader of the assault at the mine of Petersburg? The solitary horseman in front of Port Hudson, whom a foeman worthy of him bade his soldiers spare, from love and admiration of such gallant bearing? Who does not still hear the echo of those eloquent lips after the war, teaching reconciliation and peace? I may not do more than allude to his death, fit ending of his life. All that the world has a right to know has been told by a beloved friend in a book wherein friendship has found no need to exaggerate facts that speak for themselves. I knew him, and I may even say I knew him well; yet, until that book appeared, I had not known the governing motive of his soul. I had admired him as a hero. When I read, I learned to revere him as a saint. His strength was not in honor alone, but in religion; and those who do not share his creed must see that it was on the wings of religious faith that he mounted above even valiant deeds into an empyrean of ideal life.

I have spoken of some of the men who were near to me among others very near and dear, not because their lives have become historic, but because their lives are the type of what every soldier has known and seen in his own company. In the great democracy of self-devotion private and general stand side by side. Unmarshalled save by their own deeds, the armies of the dead sweep before us, "wearing their wounds like stars." It is not because the men whom I have mentioned were my friends that I have spoken of them, but, I repeat, because they are types. I speak of those whom I have seen. But you all have known such; you, too, remember!

It is not of the dead alone that we think on this day. There are those still living whose sex forbade them to offer their lives, but who gave instead their happiness. Which of us has not been lifted above himself by the sight of one of those lovely, lonely women, around whom the wand of sorrow has traced its excluding circle —set apart, even when surrounded by loving friends who would fain bring back joy to their lives? I think of one whom the poor of a great city knew as their benefactress and friend. I think of one who has lived not less greatly in the midst of her children, to whom she has taught such lessons as may not be heard elsewhere from mortal lips. The story of these and of their sisters we must pass in reverent silence. All that may be said has been said by one of their own sex:

But when the days of golden dreams had perished,
And even despair was powerless to destroy,
Then did I learn how existence could be cherished,
Strengthened, and fed without the aid of joy.

Then did I check the tears of useless passion,
Weaned my young soul from yearning after thine,
Sternly denied its burning wish to hasten
Down to that tomb already more than mine.

Comrades, some of the associations of this day are not only triumphant, but joyful. Not all of those with whom we once stood shoulder to shoulder—not all of those whom we once loved and revered—are gone. On this day we still meet our companions in the freezing winter bivouacs and in those dreadful summer marches where every faculty of the soul seemed to depart one after another, leaving only a dumb animal power to set the teeth and to persist—a blind belief that somewhere and at last there was rest and water. On this day, at least, we still meet and rejoice in the closest tie which is possible between men—a tie which suffering has made indissoluble for better, for worse.

When we meet thus, when we do honor to the dead in terms that must sometimes embrace the living, we do not deceive ourselves. We attribute no special merit to a man for having served when all were serving. We know that, if the armies of our war did anything worth remembering, the credit belongs not mainly to the individuals who did it, but to average human nature. We also know very well that we cannot live in associations with the past alone, and we admit that, if we would be worthy of the past, we must find new fields for action or thought, and make for ourselves new careers.

But, nevertheless, the generation that carried on the war has been set apart by its experience. Through our great good fortune, in our youth our hearts were touched with fire. It was given to us to learn at the outset that life is a profound and passionate thing. While we are permitted to scorn nothing but indifference, and do not pretend to undervalue the worldly rewards of ambition, we have seen with our own eyes, beyond and above the gold fields, the snowy heights of honor, and it is for us to bear the report to those who come after us. But, above all, we have learned that whether a man accepts from Fortune her spade, and will look downward and dig, or from Aspiration her axe and cord, and will scale the ice, the one and only success which it is his to command is to bring to his work a mighty heart.

Such hearts—ah me, how many!—were stilled twenty years ago; and to us who remain behind is left this day of memories. Every year—in the full tide of spring, at the height of the symphony of flowers and love and life—there comes a pause, and through the silence we hear the lonely pipe of death. Year after year lovers wandering under the apple boughs and through the clover and deep grass are surprised with sudden tears as they see black veiled figures stealing through the morning to a soldier's grave. Year after year the comrades of the dead follow, with public honor, procession and commemorative flags, and funeral march—honor and grief from us who stand almost alone, and have seen the best and noblest of our generation pass away.

But grief is not the end of all. I seem to hear the funeral march became a pæan. I see beyond the forest the moving banners of a hidden column. Our dead brothers still live for us, and bid us think of life, not death—of life to which in their youth they lent the passion and glory of the spring. As I listen, the great chorus of life and joy begins again, and amid the awful orchestra of seen and unseen powers and destinies of good and evil our trumpets sound once more a note of daring, hope, and will.

HARVARD COLLEGE IN THE WAR

Answer to a Toast at Harvard University Commencement, June 25, 1884

MR. PRESIDENT AND GENTLEMEN OF THE ALUMNI: Another day than this has been consecrated to the memories of the war. On that day we think not of the children of the University or the city, hardly even of the children whom the State has lost, but of a mighty brotherhood whose parent was our common country. To-day the College is the center of all our feeling, and if we refer to the war it is in connection with the College, and not for its own sake, that we do so. What, then, did the College do to justify our speaking of the war now? She sent a few gentlemen into the field, who died there becomingly. I know of nothing more. The great forces which insured the North success would have been at work even if those men had been absent. Our means of raising money and troops would not have been less, I dare say. The great qualities of the race, too, would still have been there. The greatest qualities, after all, are those of a man, not those of a gentleman, and neither North nor South needed colleges to learn them. And yet—and yet I think we all feel that to us at least the war would seem less beautiful and inspiring if those few gentlemen had not died as they did. Look at yonder portrait and yonder bust, and tell me if stories such as they commemorate do not add a glory to the bare fact that the strongest legions prevailed. So it has been since wars began. After history has done its best to fix men's thoughts upon strategy and finance, their eyes have turned and rested on some single romantic figure—some Sidney, some Falkland, some Wolfe, some Montcalm, some Shaw. This is that little touch of the superfluous which is necessary. Necessary as art is necessary, and knowledge which serves no mechanical end. Superfluous only as glory is superfluous, or a bit of red ribbon that a man would die to win.

It has been one merit of Harvard College that it has never quite sunk to believing that its only function was to carry a body of specialists through the first stage of their preparation. About these halls there has always been an aroma of high feeling, not to be found or lost in science or Greek—not to be fixed, yet all-pervading. And the warrant of Harvard College for writing the names of its dead graduates upon its tablets is not in the mathematics, the chemistry, the political economy, which it taught them, but that in ways not to be discovered, by traditions not to be written down, it helped men of lofty natures to make good their faculties. I hope and I believe that it long will give such help to its children. I hope and I believe that, long after we and our tears for the dead have been forgotten, this monument to their memory still will give such help to generations to whom it is only a symbol—a symbol of man's destiny and power for duty, but a symbol also of that something more by which duty is swallowed up in generosity, that something more which led men like Shaw to toss life and hope like a flower before the feet of their country and their cause.

NOTE.—The portrait referred to is that of Colonel Robert Gould Shaw, killed at Fort Wagner, South Carolina, July 18, 1863, in command of the Fifty-fourth Massachusetts Regiment (colored). The bust is that of Brigadier-General Charles Russell Lowell, died, October 20, 1864, of wounds received at Cedar Creek, Virginia, October 19.

THE LAW

Suffolk Bar Association Dinner,
February 5, 1885

MR. CHAIRMAN AND GENTLEMEN OF THE BAR: The Court and the Bar are too old acquaintances to speak much to each other of themselves, or of their mutual relations. I hope I may say we are too old friends to need to do it. If you did not believe it already, it would be useless for me to affirm that, in the judges' half of our common work, the will at least is not wanting to do every duty of their noble office; that every interest, every faculty, every energy, almost every waking hour, is filled with their work; that they give their lives to it, more than which they cannot do. But if not of the Bench, shall I speak of the Bar? Shall I ask what a court would be, unaided? The law is made by the Bar, even more than by the Bench; yet do I need to speak of the learning and varied gifts that have given the bar of this State a reputation throughout the whole domain of the common law? I think I need not, nor of its high and scrupulous honor. The world has its fling at lawyers sometimes, but its very denial is an admission. It feels, what I believe to be the truth, that of all secular professions this has the highest standards.

And what a profession it is! No doubt everything is interesting when it is understood and seen in its connection with the rest of things. Every calling is great when greatly pursued. But what other gives such scope to realize the spontaneous energy of one's soul? In what other does one plunge so deep in the stream of life—so share its passions, its battles, its despair, its triumphs, both as witness and actor?

But that is not all. What a subject is this in which we are united—this abstraction called the Law, wherein, as in a magic mirror, we see reflected, not only our own lives, but the lives of all men that have been! When I think on this majestic theme, my eyes dazzle. If we are to speak of the law as our mistress, we who are here know that she is a mistress only to be wooed with sustained and lonely passion—only to be won by straining all the faculties by which man is likest to a god. Those who, having begun the pursuit, turn away uncharmed, do so either because they have not been vouchsafed the sight of her divine figure, or because they have not the heart for so great a struggle. To the lover of the law, how small a thing seem the novelist's tales of the loves and fates of Daphnis and Chloe! How pale a phantom even the Circe of poetry, transforming mankind with intoxicating dreams of fiery ether, and the foam of summer seas, and glowing greensward, and the white arms of women! For him no less a history will suffice than that of the moral life of his race. For him every text that he deciphers, every doubt that he resolves, adds a new feature to the unfolding panorama of man's destiny upon this earth. Nor will his task be done until, by the farthest stretch of human imagination, he has seen as with his eyes the birth and growth of society, and by the farthest stretch of reason he has understood the philosophy of its being. When I think thus of the law, I see a princess mightier than she who once wrought at Bayeux, eternally weaving into her web dim figures of the ever-lengthening past—figures too dim to be noticed by the idle, too symbolic to be interpreted except by her pupils, but to the discerning eye disclosing every painful step and every world-shaking contest by which mankind has worked and fought its way from savage isolation to organic social life.

But we who are here know the Law even better in another aspect. We see her daily, not as anthropologists, not as students and philosophers, but as actors in a drama of which she is the providence and overruling power. When I think of the Law as we know her in the courthouse and the market, she seems to me a woman sitting by the wayside, beneath whose overshadowing hood every man shall see the countenance of his deserts or needs. The timid and overborne gain heart from her protecting smile. Fair combatants, manfully standing to their rights, see her keeping the lists with the stern and discriminating eye of even justice. The wretch who has defied her most sacred commands, and has thought to creep through ways where she was not, finds that his path ends with her, and beholds beneath her hood the inexorable face of death.

Gentlemen, I shall say no more. This is not the moment for disquisitions. But when for the first time I was called to speak on such an occasion as this, the only thought that could come into my mind, the only feeling that could fill my heart, the only words that could spring to my lips, were a hymn to her in whose name we are met here to-night—to our mistress, the Law.

THE PURITAN

250th Anniversary of the First Church in Cambridge, February 12, 1886

MR. CHAIRMAN AND GENTLEMEN: Six hundred years ago a knight went forth to fight for the cross in Palestine. He fought his battles, returned, died among his friends, and his effigy, cut in alabaster or cast in bronze, was set upon his tomb in the Temple or the Abbey. Already he was greater than he had been in life. While he lived, hundreds as good as he fell beneath the walls of Ascalon, or sank in the sands of the desert and were forgotten. But in his monument, the knight became the type of chivalry and the church militant. What was particular to him and individual had passed from sight, and the universal alone remained. Six hundred years have gone by, and his history, perhaps his very name, has been forgotten. His cause has ceased to move. The tumultuous tide in which he was an atom is still. And yet to-day he is greater than ever before. He is no longer a man, or even the type of a class of men, however great. He has become a symbol of the whole mysterious past—of all the dead passion of his race. His monument is the emblem of tradition, the text of national honor, the torch of all high aspiration through all time.

The Puritan

Two hundred and fifty years ago a few devout men founded the First Church of Cambridge. While they lived, I doubt not, hundreds as good as they fell under Fairfax at Marston Moor, or under Cromwell at Naseby, or lived and died quietly in England and were forgotten. Yet if the only monuments of those founders were mythic bronzes, such as stand upon the Common and the Delta—if they were only the lichened slates in yonder churchyard—how much greater are they now than they were in life! Time, the purifier, has burned away what was particular to them and individual, and has left only the type of courage, constancy, devotion—the august figure of the Puritan.

Time still burns. Perhaps the type of the Puritan must pass away, as that of the Crusader has done. But the founders of this parish are commemorated, not in bronze or alabaster, but in living monuments. One is Harvard College. The other is mightier still. These men and their fellows planted a congregational church, from which grew a democratic state. They planted something mightier even than institutions. Whether they knew it or not, they planted the democratic spirit in the heart of man. It is to them we owe the deepest cause we have to love our country—that instinct, that spark that makes the American unable to meet his fellow man otherwise than simply as a man, eye to eye, hand to hand, and foot to foot, wrestling naked on the sand. When the citizens of Cambridge forget that they too tread a sacred soil, that Massachusetts also has its traditions, which grow more venerable and inspiring as they fade—when Harvard College is no longer dedicated to truth, and America to democratic freedom—then perhaps, but not till then, will the blood of the martyrs be swallowed in the sand, and the Puritan have lived in vain. Until that time he will grow greater, even after he has vanished from our view.

The political children of Thomas Shepard we surely are. We are not all his spiritual children. New England has welcomed and still welcomes to her harbors many who are not the Puritan's descendants, and his descendants have learned other ways and other thoughts than those in which he lived and for which he was ready to die. I confess that my own interest in those thoughts is chiefly filial; that it seems to me that the great currents of the world's life ran in other channels, and that the future lay in the heads of Bacon and Hobbes and Descartes, rather even than in that of John Milton. I think that the somewhat isolated thread of our intellectual and spiritual life is rejoining the main stream, and that hereafter all countries more and more will draw from common springs.

But even if we are not all of us the spiritual children of Thomas Shepard, even if our mode of expressing our wonder, our awful fear, our abiding trust in face of life and death and the unfathomable world has changed, yet at this day, even now, we New Englanders are still leavened with the Puritan ferment. Our doctrines may have changed, but the cold Puritan passion is still here. And of many a man who now hears me, whether a member of his church or not, it may be said, as it was said of Thomas Shepard by Cotton Mather, "So the character of his daily conversation was a trembling walk with God."

NOTE.—Thomas Shepard was the first minister of the First Church in Cambridge. My grandfather, Rev. Abiel Holmes, was minister of it in his day.

THE PROFESSION OF THE LAW

Conclusion of a Lecture Delivered to Undergraduates of Harvard University, on February 17, 1886

And now, perhaps, I ought to have done. But I know that some spirit of fire will feel that his main question has not been answered. He will ask, What is all this to my soul? You do not bid me sell my birthright for a mess of pottage; what have you said to show that I can reach my own spiritual possibilities through such a door as this? How can the laborious study of a dry and technical system, the greedy watch for clients and practice of shopkeepers' arts, the mannerless conflicts over often sordid interests, make out a life? Gentlemen, I admit at once that these questions are not futile, that they may prove unanswerable, that they have often seemed to me unanswerable. And yet I believe there is an answer. They are the same questions that meet you in any form of practical life. If a man has the soul of Sancho Panza, the world to him will be Sancho Panza's world; but if he has the soul of an idealist, he will make—I do not say find—his world ideal. Of course, the law is not the place for the artist or the poet. The law is the calling of thinkers. But to those who believe with me that not the least godlike of man's activities is the large survey of causes, that to know is not less than to feel, I say—and I say no longer with any doubt—that a man may live greatly in the law as well as elsewhere; that there as well as elsewhere his thought may find its unity in an infinite perspective; that there as well as elsewhere he may wreak himself upon life, may drink the bitter cup of heroism, may wear his heart out after the unattainable. All that life offers any man from which to start his thinking or his striving is a fact. And if this universe is one universe, if it is so far thinkable that you can pass in reason from one part of it to another, it does not matter very much what that fact is. For every fact leads to every other by the path of the air. Only men do not yet see how, always. And your business as thinkers is to make plainer the way from some thing to the whole of things; to show the rational connection between your fact and the frame of the universe. If your subject is law, the roads are plain to anthropology, the science of man, to political economy, the theory of legislation, ethics, and thus by several paths to your final view of life. It would be equally true of any subject. The only difference is in the ease of seeing the way. To be master of any branch of knowledge, you must master those which lie next to it; and thus to know anything you must know all.

Perhaps I speak too much the language of intellectual ambition. I cannot but think that the scope for intellectual, as for physical adventure, is narrowing. I look for a future in which the ideal will be content and dignified acceptance of life, rather than aspiration and the passion for achievement. I see already that surveys and railroads have set limits to our intellectual wildernesses—that the lion and the bison are disappearing from them, as from Africa and the no longer boundless West. But that undelightful day which I anticipate has not yet come. The human race has not changed, I imagine, so much between my generation and yours but that you still have the barbaric thirst for conquest, and there is still something left to conquer. There are fields still open for occupation in the law, and there are roads from them that will lead you where you will.

But do not think I am pointing you to flowery paths and beds of roses—to a place where brilliant results attend your work, which shall be at once easy and new. No result is easy which is worth having. Your education begins when what is called your education is over—when you no longer are stringing together the pregnant thoughts, the "jewels five words long," which great men have given their lives to cut from the raw material, but have begun yourselves to work upon the raw material for results which you do not see, cannot predict, and which may be long in coming—when you take the fact which life offers you for your appointed task. No man has earned the right to intellectual ambition until he has learned to lay his course by a star which he has never seen—to dig by the divining rod for springs which he may never reach. In saying this, I point to that which will make your study heroic. For I say to you in all sadness of conviction, that to think great thoughts you must be heroes as well as idealists. Only when you have worked alone—when you have felt around you a black gulf of solitude more isolating than that which surrounds the dying man, and in hope and in despair have trusted to your own unshaken will—then only will you have achieved. Thus only can you gain the secret isolated joy of the thinker, who knows that, a hundred years after he is dead and forgotten, men who never heard of him will be moving to the measure of his thought—the subtile rapture of a postponed power, which the world knows not because it has no external trappings, but which to his prophetic vision is more real than that which commands an army. And if this joy should not be yours, still it is only thus that you can know that you have done what it lay in you to do—can say that you have lived, and be ready for the end.

ON RECEIVING THE DEGREE OF DOCTOR OF LAWS

Yale University Commencement, June 30, 1886

Mr. President and Gentlemen: I know of no mark of honor which this country has to offer that I should value so highly as this which you have conferred upon me. I accept it proudly as an accolade, like the little blow upon the shoulder from the sword of a master of war which in ancient days adjudged that a soldier had won his spurs and pledged his life to decline no combat in the future.

The power of honor to bind men's lives is not less now than it was in the Middle Ages. Now as then it is the breath of our nostrils; it is that for which we live, for which, if need be, we are willing to die. It is that which makes the man whose gift is the power to gain riches sacrifice health and even life to the pursuit. It is that which makes the scholar feel that he cannot afford to be rich.

One would sometimes think, from the speech of young men, that things had changed recently, and that indifference was now the virtue to be cultivated. I never heard any one profess indifference to a boat race. Why should you row a boat race? Why endure long months of pain in preparation for a fierce half-hour that will leave you all but dead? Does any one ask the question? Is there any one who would not go through all its costs, and more, for the moment when anguish breaks into triumph —or even for the glory of having nobly lost? Is life less than a boat race? If a man will give all the blood in his body to win the one, will he not spend all the might of his soul to prevail in the other?

I know, Mr. President, that there is a motive above even honor which may govern men's lives. I know that there are some rare spirits who find the inspiration of every moment, the aim of every act, in holiness. I am enough of a Puritan, I think, to conceive the exalted joy of those who look upon themselves only as instruments in the hands of a higher power to work out its designs. But I think that most men do and must reach the same result under the illusion of self-seeking. If the love of honor is a form of that illusion, it is no ignoble one. If it does not lift a man on wings to the sky, at least it carries him above the earth and teaches him those high and secret pathways across the branches of the forest the travelers on which are only less than winged.

Not the least service of this great University and its sister from which I come is, that by their separate teaching and by their mutual rivalry they have fostered that lofty feeling among their graduates. You have done all that a university can do to fan the spark in me. I will try to maintain the honor you have bestowed.

THE USE OF LAW SCHOOLS

Oration Before the Harvard Law School Association, at Cambridge, November 5, 1886, on the 250th Anniversary of Harvard University

It is not wonderful that the graduates of the Law School of Harvard College should wish to keep alive their connection with it. About three quarters of a century ago it began with a Chief Justice of the Supreme Court of Massachusetts for its Royall Professor. A little later, one of the most illustrious judges who ever sat on the United States Supreme Bench—Mr. Justice Story—accepted a professorship in it created for him by Nathan Dane. And from that time to this it has had the services of great and famous lawyers; it has been the source of a large part of the most important legal literature which the country has produced; it has furnished a world-renowned model in its modes of instruction; and it has had among its students future chief justices and justices, and leaders of state bars and of the national bar too numerous for me to thrill you with the mention of their names.

It has not taught great lawyers only. Many who have won fame in other fields began their studies here. Sumner and Phillips were among the Bachelors of 1834. The orator whom we shall hear in a day or two appears in the list of 1840 alongside of William Story, of the Chief Justice of this State, and of one of the Associate Justices, who is himself not less known as a soldier and as an orator than he is as a judge. Perhaps, without revealing family secrets, I may whisper that next Monday's poet also tasted our masculine diet before seeking more easily digested, if not more nutritious, food elsewhere. Enough. Of course we are proud of the Harvard Law School. Of course we love every limb of Harvard College. Of course we rejoice to manifest our brotherhood by the symbol of this Association.

I will say no more for the reasons of our coming together. But by your leave I will say a few words about the use and meaning of law schools, especially of our law school, and about its methods of instruction, as they appear to one who has had some occasion to consider them.

A law school does not undertake to teach success. That combination of tact and will which gives a man immediate prominence among his fellows comes from nature, not from instruction; and if it can be helped at all by advice, such advice is not offered here. It might be expected that I should say, by way of natural antithesis, that what a law school does undertake to teach is law. But I am not ready to say even that, without a qualification. It seems to me that nearly all the education which men can get from others is moral, not intellectual. The main part of intellectual education is not the acquisition of facts, but learning how to make facts live. Culture, in the sense of fruitless knowledge, I for one abhor. The mark of a master is, that facts which before lay scattered in an inorganic mass, when he shoots through them the magnetic current of his thought, leap into an organic order, and live and bear fruit. But you cannot make a master by teaching. He makes himself by aid of his natural gifts.

Education, other than self-education, lies mainly in the shaping of men's interests and aims. If you convince a man that another way of looking at things is more profound, another form of pleasure more subtile than that to which he has been accustomed—if you make him really see it—the very nature of man is such that he will desire the profounder thought and the subtiler joy. So I say the business of a law school is not sufficiently described when you merely say that it is to teach law, or to make lawyers. It is to teach law in the grand manner, and to make great lawyers.

Our country needs such teaching very much. I think we should all agree that the passion for equality has passed far beyond the political or even the social sphere. We are not only unwilling to admit that any class or society is better than that in which we move, but our customary attitude towards every one in authority of any kind is that he is only the lucky recipient of honor or salary above the average, which any average man might as well receive as he. When the effervescence of democratic negation extends its workings beyond the abolition of external distinctions of rank to spiritual things—when the passion for equality is not content with founding social intercourse upon universal human sympathy, and a community of interests in which all may share, but attacks the lines of Nature which establish orders and degrees among the souls of men—they are not only wrong, but ignobly wrong. Modesty and reverence are no less virtues of freemen than the democratic feeling which will submit neither to arrogance nor to servility.

To inculcate those virtues, to correct the ignoble excess of a noble feeling to which I have referred, I know of no teachers so powerful and persuasive as the little army of specialists. They carry no banners, they beat no drums; but where they are, men learn that bustle and push are not the equals of quiet genius and serene mastery. They compel others who need their help, or who are enlightened by their teaching, to obedience and respect. They set the example themselves; for they furnish in the intellectual world a perfect type of the union of democracy with discipline. They bow to no one who seeks to impose his authority by foreign aid; they hold that science like courage is never beyond the necessity of proof, but must always be ready to prove itself against all challengers. But to one who has shown himself a master, they pay the proud reverence of men who know what valiant combat means, and who reserve the right of combat against their leader even, if he should seem to waver in the service of Truth, their only queen.

In the army of which I speak, the lawyers are not the least important corps. For all lawyers are specialists. Not in the narrow sense in which we sometimes use the word in the profession—of persons who confine themselves to a particular branch of practice, such as conveyancing or patents—but specialists who have taken all law to be their province; specialists because they have undertaken to master a special branch of human knowledge—a branch, I may add, which is more immediately connected with all the highest interests of man than any other which deals with practical affairs.

Lawyers, too, were among the first specialists to be needed and to appear in America. And I believe it would be hard to exaggerate the goodness of their influence in favor of sane and orderly thinking. But lawyers feel the spirit of the times like other people. They, like others, are forever trying to discover cheap and agreeable substitutes for real things. I fear that the bar has done its full share to exalt that most hateful of American words and ideals, "smartness," as against dignity of moral feeling and profundity of knowledge. It is from within the bar, not from outside, that I have heard the new gospel that learning is out of date, and that the man for the times is no longer the thinker and the scholar, but the smart man, unencumbered with other artillery than the latest edition of the Digest and the latest revision of the Statutes.

The aim of a law school should be, the aim of the Harvard Law School has been, not to make men smart, but to make them wise in their calling—to start them on a road which will lead them to the abode of the masters. A law school should be at once the workshop and the nursery of specialists in the sense which I have explained. It should obtain for teachers men in each generation who are producing the best work of that generation. Teaching should not stop, but rather should foster, production. The "enthusiasm of the lecture-room," the contagious interest of companionship, should make the students partners in their teachers' work. The ferment of genius in its creative moment is quickly imparted. If a man is great, he makes others believe in greatness; he makes them incapable of mean ideals and easy self-satisfaction. His pupils will accept no substitute for realities; but at the same time they learn that the only coin with which realities can be bought is Life.

Our School has been such a workshop and such a nursery as I describe. What men it has turned out I have hinted already, and do not need to say; what works it has produced is known to all the world. From ardent co-operation of student and teacher have sprung Greenleaf on Evidence, and Stearns on Real Actions, and Story's epoch-making Commentaries, and Parsons on Contracts, and Washburn on Real Property; and, marking a later epoch, Langdell on Contracts and on Equity Pleading, and Ames on Bills and Notes, and Gray on Perpetuities, and I hope we may soon add Thayer on Evidence. You will notice that these books are very different in character from one another, but you will notice also how many of them have this in common—that they have marked and largely made an epoch.

There are plenty of men nowadays of not a hundredth part of Story's power who could write as good statements of the law as his, or better. And when some mediocre fluent book has been printed, how often have we heard it proclaimed, "Lo, here is a greater than Story!" But if you consider the state of legal literature when Story began to write, and from what wells of learning the discursive streams of his speech were fed, I think you will be inclined to agree with me that he has done more than any other English-speaking man in this century to make the law luminous and easy to understand.

But Story's simple philosophizing has ceased to satisfy men's minds. I think it might be said with safety, that no man of his or of the succeeding generation could have stated the law in a form that deserved to abide, because neither his nor the succeeding generation possessed or could have possessed the historical knowledge, had made or could have made the analyses of principles, which are necessary before the cardinal doctrines of the law can be known and understood in their precise contours and in their innermost meanings.

The new work is now being done. Under the influence of Germany, science is gradually drawing legal history into its sphere. The facts are being scrutinized by eyes microscopic in intensity and panoramic in scope. At the same time, under the influence of our revived interest in philosophical speculation, a thousand heads are analyzing and generalizing the rules of law and the grounds on which they stand. The law has got to be stated over again; and I venture to say that in fifty years we shall have it in a form of which no man could have dreamed fifty years ago. And now I venture to add my hope and my belief, that, when the day comes which I predict, the Professors of the Harvard Law School will be found to have had a hand in the change not less important than that which Story has had in determining the form of the text-books of the last half-century.

Corresponding to the change which I say is taking place, there has been another change in the mode of teaching. How far the correspondence is conscious, I do not stop to inquire. For whatever reason, the Professors of this School have said to themselves more definitely than ever before, We will not be contented to send forth students with nothing but a rag-bag full of general principles—a throng of glittering generalities, like a swarm of little bodiless cherubs fluttering at the top of one of Corregio's pictures. They have said that to make a general principle worth anything you must give it a body; you must show in what way and how far it would be applied actually in an actual system; you must show how it has gradually emerged as the felt reconciliation of concrete instances no one of which established it in terms. Finally, you must show its historic relations to other principles, often of very different date and origin, and thus set it in the perspective without which its proportions will never be truly judged.

In pursuance of these views there have been substituted for text-books more and more, so far as practicable, those books of cases which were received at first by many with a somewhat contemptuous smile and pitying contrast of the good old days, but which now, after fifteen years, bid fair to revolutionize the teaching both of this country and of England.

I pause for a moment to say what I hope it is scarcely necessary for me to say—that in thus giving in my adhesion to the present methods of instruction I am not wanting in grateful and appreciative recollection (alas! it can be only recollection now) of the earlier teachers under whom I studied. In my day the Dean of this School was Professor Parker, the ex-Chief Justice of New Hampshire, who I think was one of the greatest of American judges, and who showed in the chair the same qualities that had made him famous on the bench. His associates were Parsons, almost if not quite a man of genius, and gifted with a power of impressive statement which I do not know that I have ever seen equalled; and Washburn, who taught us all to realize the meaning of the phrase which I already have quoted from Vangerow, the "enthusiasm of the lecture-room." He did more for me than the learning of Coke and the logic of Fearne could have done without his kindly ardor.

To return, and to say a word more about the theory on which these books of cases are used. It long has seemed to me a striking circumstance, that the ablest of the agitators for codification, Sir James Stephen, and the originator of the present mode of teaching, Mr. Langdell, start from the same premises to reach seemingly opposite conclusions. The number of legal principles is small, says in effect Sir James Stephen, therefore codify them; the number of legal principles is small, says Mr. Langdell, therefore they may be taught through the cases which have developed and established them. Well, I think there is much force in Sir James Stephen's argument, if you can find competent men and get them to undertake the task; and at any rate I am not now going to express an opinion that he is wrong. But I am certain from my own experience that Mr. Langdell is right; I am certain that when your object is not to make a bouquet of the law for the public, nor to prune and graft it by legislation, but to plant its roots where they will grow, in minds devoted henceforth to that one end, there is no way to be compared to Mr. Langdell's way. Why, look at it simply in the light of human nature. Does not a man remember a concrete instance more vividly than a general principle? And is not a principle more exactly and intimately grasped as the unexpressed major premise of the half-dozen examples which mark its extent and its limits than it can be in any abstract form of words? Expressed or unexpressed, is it not better known when you have studied its embryology and the lines of its growth than when you merely see it lying dead before you on the printed page?

I have referred to my own experience. During the short time that I had the honor of teaching in the School, it fell to me, among other things, to instruct the first-year men in Torts. With some misgivings I plunged a class of beginners straight into Mr. Ames's collection of cases, and we began to discuss them together in Mr. Langdell's method. The result was better than I even hoped it would be. After a week or two, when the first confusing novelty was over, I found that my class examined the questions proposed with an accuracy of view which they never could have learned from text-books, and which often exceeded that to be found in the text-books. I at least, if no one else, gained a good deal from our daily encounters.

My experience as a judge has confirmed the belief I formed as a professor. Of course a young man cannot try or argue a case as well as one who has had years of experience. Most of you also would probably agree with me that no teaching which a man receives from others at all approaches in importance what he does for himself, and that one who simply has been a docile pupil has got but a very little way. But I do think that in the thoroughness of their training, and in the systematic character of their knowledge, the young men of the present day start better equipped when they begin their practical experience than it was possible for their predecessors to have been. And although no school can boast a monopoly of promising young men, Cambridge, of course, has its full proportion of them at our bar; and I do think that the methods of teaching here bear fruits in their work.

I sometimes hear a wish expressed by the impatient, that the teaching here should be more practical. I remember that a very wise and able man said to a friend of mine when he was beginning his professional life, "Don't know too much law," and I think we all can imagine cases where the warning would be useful. But a far more useful thing is what was said to me as a student by one no less wise and able—afterwards my partner and always my friend—when I was talking as young men do about seeing practice, and all the other things which seemed practical to my inexperience, "The business of a lawyer is to know law." The Professors of this Law School mean to make their students know law. They think the most practical teaching is that which takes their students to the bottom of what they seek to know. They therefore mean to make them master the common law and equity as working systems, and think that when that is accomplished they will have no trouble with the improvements of the last half-century. I believe they are entirely right, not only in the end they aim at, but in the way they take to reach that end.

Yes, this School has been, is, and I hope long will be, a center where great lawyers perfect their achievements, and from which young men, even more inspired by their example than instructed by their teaching, go forth in their turn, not to imitate what their masters have done, but to live their own lives more freely for the ferment imparted to them here. The men trained in this School may not always be the most knowing in the ways of getting on. The noblest of them must often feel that they are committed to lives of proud dependence—the dependence of men who command no factitious aids to success, but rely upon unadvertised knowledge and silent devotion; dependence upon finding an appreciation which they cannot seek, but dependence proud in the conviction that the knowledge to which their lives are consecrated is of things which it concerns the world to know. It is the dependence of abstract thought, of science, of beauty, of poetry and art, of every flower of civilization, upon finding a soil generous enough to support it. If it does not, it must die. But the world needs the flower more than the flower needs life.

I said that a law school ought to teach law in the grand manner; that it had something more to do than simply to teach law. I think we may claim for our School that it has not been wanting in greatness. I once heard a Russian say that in the middle class of Russia there were many specialists; in the upper class there were civilized men. Perhaps in America, for reasons which I have mentioned, we need specialists even more than we do civilized men. Civilized men who are nothing else are a little apt to think that they cannot breathe the American atmosphere. But if a man is a specialist, it is most desirable that he should also be civilized; that he should have laid in the outline of the other sciences, as well as the light and shade of his own; that he should be reasonable, and see things in their proportion. Nay, more, that he should be passionate, as well as reasonable—that he should be able not only to explain, but to feel; that the ardors of intellectual pursuit should be relieved by the charms of art, should be succeeded by the joy of life become an end in itself.

At Harvard College is realized in some degree the palpitating manifoldness of a truly civilized life. Its apirations are concealed because they are chastened and instructed; but I believe in my soul that they are not the less noble that they are silent. The golden light of the University is not confined to the undergraduate department; it is shed over all the schools. He who has once seen it becomes other than he was, forevermore. I have said that the best part of our education is moral. It is the crowning glory of this Law School that it has kindled in many a heart an inextinguishable fire.

NOTE.—The orator referred to was James Russell Lowell; the poet was Oliver Wendell Holmes.

REMARKS TO THE ESSEX BAR

GENTLEMEN OF THE ESSEX BAR: You remember the lions of the Twentieth and the Second at the foot of the grand staircase in the Public Library of Boston. If they had been consecrated to the soldiers of the city in general they would have moved us less, still less if to the soldiers of the State, and if to valor in the abstract they would have moved us not at all. If you want to reach men's hearts you must deal with things and persons, not with abstractions. On the same principle the nearest motive for good conduct is found in the opinion of neighbors and friends, not in the generalities of abstract rules. I suppose that if fifty years ago a skipper from Gloucester or Marblehead went down at his moorings on the Banks rather than lose a shot of cable, the thought of what they would say on winter evenings in the grocery store counted for more than any reflections upon the greatest good of the greatest number. And it is still on the same principle that I heartily believe in organizations like this and other County Bar Associations which start from

SOURCE: an undated, typed copy, with corrections in Holmes's hand, preserved among the Holmes papers at the Harvard Law School. The date of delivery of the remarks has not been ascertained. Mr. Justice Lord, of the Supreme Judicial Court, who is referred to in the remarks, died in 1884. It is likely that Holmes made his remarks at an annual meeting of the Essex Bar Association. Those meetings normally occurred in December.

ties already formed in acquaintance and neighborhood and the brotherhood of fight.

Nevertheless, isolation is but a stage. It is not the end. Nothing is or can be isolated, as we all know, although we do not always keep it in mind. Our planets and our sun make a comfortable little constellation of their own, but they cannot escape from the bonds of that vaster association in which they sweep along with all the rest to the "divine far-off event." Our country has avoided entangling alliances, but it is bound to the other nations more and more closely by wire and rail and steamer, by commerce, yes, and by sympathy, as the world grows more and more one. So it is with everything in its degree. A fact taken by itself is gossip, seen in its connections and relations it is part of science and philosophy. So with the law. So with the practice of every one of you. You argue a case in Essex. And what has the world outside to do with that, you say. Yet you have confirmed or modified or perhaps have suggested for the first time a principle which will find its way into the reports and from the reports into the text-books and so into the thought of the common law, and so into its share in governing the conduct of civilized men. Our every act rings through the whole world of being.

I think that we need to bear in mind this high, universal significance of our work even more than to renew and fortify our parochial brotherhoods. The thought of it is our highest inspiration. For it bids us count for as much as we can in shaping what is to come. It also is our severest critic. For it demands that if we would affect civilization we should be civilized—that in argument or decision we should have the courage to take the well known for granted—that we should come at once to the precise discrimination upon which we rely, stating that with all the refinement that we can master, indicating, it may be, its roots in history or principle, but shunning as we would shun intellectual death the platitudes which, so far as true, are well known and carry us only to the beginning of the particular task in hand. The bench and the Bar have the right to expect of each other that they should assume their discourse to be directed to masters of the business. If we act up to that expectation I see no reason why Massachusetts should not maintain the high place which she has held so long as one of the fountains of the common law. Massachusetts did not die with Shaw, nor Essex County with Parsons or Choate or Story or Lord. Every morning the bugles blow the reveille anew, and thus far there never have been wanting soldiers or generals competent for the battle of the day.

SIDNEY BARTLETT

Answer to Resolutions of the Bar,
Boston, March 23, 1889

Gentlemen of the Bar: Your resolutions do not at all exaggerate the feelings which the Bench share with the Bar, and no one, I am sure, more than I, although my knowledge of Mr. Bartlett professionally is of a date which would seem late to some of you. When I came to the bar, Mr. Bartlett already had nearly completed his threescore and ten years, so that of what would have been his whole career, had he been another man, I cannot speak. I have, however, one reminiscence which I cherish, and which takes us back in imagination beyond the oldest memory. I hold in my hand a letter in which he says, "Deacon Spooner died in 1818 aged ninety-four. I saw him and talked with him. *He* talked with Elder Faunce, who talked with the Pilgrims and is said to have pointed out *the* rock."

It is not necessary to go behind what I can remember myself to bear witness to a great career. Between seventy and ninety Mr. Bartlett did work enough for the glory of an advocate's lifetime. I will not stop to mention famous cases, like that of the Merchants' Bank with the Government and the State Bank, or that of the Credit

Mobilier, or other cases connected with the Union Pacific, but will rather repeat what no doubt has been mentioned at your meeting, that the judges of the Supreme Court of the United States pronounced his arguments the ablest which they heard from any man in the country, and that the memory of one of those who thus spoke of him went back to the days of Webster.

Less than two months ago he argued two cases at this bar with almost unabated fire. I suppose that those who were most familiar with his methods would point out as one secret of his success the fact that from the first instant that he was retained he began to shape his case with reference to its remotest ends. He possessed the facts when another would not yet have anticipated a controversy. He took the evidence himself, having in view the principles of law upon which he expected finally to rest his case. You could mark his advent in a cause in the course of which he had been retained merely by reading the record.

But the day when he shone was when he came to argue the questions of law. His way of disregarding ramifications and cutting at the root alone you all remember too well to make description necessary. If I were asked to say what seemed to me his most striking characteristic, I think I should say *style*—taking that word in a large sense. In that respect he often made me think of the eighteenth century, which sent him down to us. He had that terse and polished subtilty of speech which was most familiar to the world where courtiers and men of fashion taught the *littérateurs* of a later age how to write. He had something of the half-hidden wit which men learned to practice who lived about a court and had to speak in innuendo. He had much of the eighteenth century definiteness of view which was such an aid to perfection of form.

His manner was no less a study than his language. There was in it a dramatic intensity of interest which made him seem the youngest man in the room when he spoke. And yet you felt at the same time the presence of something older than the oldest—the detachment which came from ancient experience and intellect undisturbed; the doubt which smiled at action without making it less ardent or sicklying o'er the native hue of resolution. His might was written in his face—that wonderful silver-crowned countenance, glittering yet serene, framed on slanting, deep-cut lines of power—the imperial face of one who had lived beyond surprises, not unlike that of the great Cæsar as Pontifex Maximus in ironic fullness of knowledge, such as still sometimes is produced in New England. It was enough to look upon him to know that you saw a man who had greatness in him.

I do not share the regrets which some are inclined to feel that Mr. Bartlett confined himself strictly to his profession. I think that he was wise in his ambition, and that his life served public ends. It seems to me that we are apt to take short-sighted views of what constitutes power, and of how a man may serve his fellows. The external and immediate result of an advocate's work is but to win or lose a case. But remotely what the lawyer does is to establish, develop, or illuminate rules which are to govern the conduct of men for centuries; to set in motion principles and influences which shape the thought and action of generations which know not by whose command they move. The man of action has the present, but the thinker controls the future; his is the most subtile, the most far-reaching power. His ambition is the vastest, as it is the most ideal.

It seems to me further that the rule for serving our fellow men, and, so far as we may speculate or hope upon that awful theme, the rule for fulfilling the mysterious ends of the universe—it seems to me that the beginning of self-sacrifice and of holiness—is to do one's task with one's might. If we do that, I think we find that our motives take care of themselves. We find that what may have been begun as a means becomes an end in itself; that self-seeking is forgotten in labors which are the best contribution that we can make to mankind; that our personality is swallowed up in working to ends outside ourselves. I, for one, am glad that our famous leader never sought the more obvious forms of power or public service, and was content to remain to the close Mr. Bartlett of the Suffolk Bar.

When a great tree falls, we are surprised to see how meager the landscape seems without it. So when a great man dies. We may not have been intimate with him; it is enough that he was within our view; when he is gone, life seems thinner and less interesting. More than that, just as, when the fire swept the ground of our city to the water's edge, we were surprised to see close at hand the ocean, which before was hidden from our vision and our thoughts, the death of this powerful bulwark against time lays open for a moment to our gaze the horizon into which we are to sail so soon. We are another generation. Our tasks are new. We shall carry different freight. The happiest of us hardly can hope for a destiny so complete and fortunate as that which has just been fulfilled. We shall be fortunate enough if we shall have learned to look into the face of fate and the unknown with a smile like his.

The resolutions of the Bar will be entered upon the records of the Court, and in token of respect to the memory of Mr. Bartlett the Court will now adjourn.

DANIEL S. RICHARDSON

Answer to Resolutions of the Bar,
Lowell, April 15, 1890

GENTLEMEN OF THE BAR: Of the leader whom you have lost I must say, *Vidi tantum*, I have seen him, and but little more. While I was at the bar, I never met him, and for the last eight years he has been rather one of the heroes of Valhalla than in the thick of daily conflict. But I have heard enough, before listening to the eloquent and touching words of those who were his friendly rivals —I might almost say I have seen enough—to know something of his character. He was a just, brave, tender, charitable, single-minded man. The men of a younger generation, who were often indebted to him for advice and opportunity freely given, bear witness to his generosity. Their elders, who knew him as an opponent rather than as a benefactor, testify to his unruffled nature, which it was not safe to disturb too nearly. He was a lover of learning, and he had that union of acuteness, judgment, and human feeling that makes a successful lawyer. He was able, wise, and good, and his being so not only brought his reward in success and affectionate regard, but, I am persuaded, did a very great deal to lift up and maintain the character of the bar to which he belonged.

His long career is spanned by the reports between the seventh of Metcalf and one of our latest volumes. It is strange to think of that monotonous series as a record of human lives. I have seen upon the section of an ancient tree the annual rings marked off which grew while the Black Prince was fighting the French, while Shakespeare wrote his plays, while England was a Commonwealth, while a later republic arose over the western waters, and grew so great as to shake the world. And so, I often think, may all our histories be marked off upon the backs of the unbroken series of our reports. As we go down the long line—at every step, as on the Appian Way, a tomb—we can see the little space within which Mason rose, grew mighty, and was no more—or Dexter, or Choate, or Bartlett, or Lord, or Sweetser. Alas! now we must add, or Richardson. And the record which remains of them is but the names of counsel attached to a few cases.

Is that the only record? I think not. Their true monument is the body of our jurisprudence—that vast cenotaph shaped by the genius of our race, and by powers greater than the greatest individual, yet to which the least may make their contribution and inscribe it with their names. The glory of lawyers, like that of men of science, is more corporate than individual. Our labor is an endless organic process. The organism whose being is recorded and protected by the law is the undying body of society. When I hear that one of the builders has ceased his toil, I do not ask what statue he has placed upon some conspicuous pedestal, but I think of the mighty whole, and say to myself, He has done his part to help the mysterious growth of the world along its inevitable lines towards its unknown end. I say to myself to-day, that all this wonder is the work of such patient, accurate, keen, just, and fearless spirits as Daniel Richardson.

The memorial will be entered upon the records of the Court as moved, and as a mark of respect to the deceased the Court will now adjourn.

ANONYMITY AND ACHIEVEMENT

Remarks at a Dinner of the Alumni of the Boston University Law School, June 3, 1890

[JUDGE HOLMES in opening his remarks alluded to the comment of some French novelist who had spoken slightingly of those who busied themselves in writing codes in bad French or upon legislation which fifty years afterward was forgotten, when another man wrote an epigram two lines long which was to be remembered and repeated for two thousand years. The novelist's moral of course was how much greater the man of literature is than the jurist, Horace than Ulpian, Musset than Savigny, and his assumed test was the length of time one's name is remembered by the general public.] He set me thinking, of some things which a lawyer has to remember, no matter what his aims or career, and which he must believe with passionate faith if his ambition is as abstract and lofty as that of the artist who fails to understand him. The greater part of the work of the world is anonymous work; the greatest displays of intellect, force of character, and power of divination are shown, for the most

SOURCE: a newspaper clipping, supplemented in Holmes's hand, preserved among the Holmes papers at the Harvard Law School.

part, in connection with private interests and are known to few beyond those immediately concerned. Even in matters of general import we owe vastly more to the forgotten than to the remembered. Think of the toil and genius in the past that have gone to making the present. It matters not whether you consider mechanical devices or the mighty structure of business, or institutions, or law, or language, or abstract ideas; on every side we live environed by the work of great minds, work a thousand-fold more important and better remembered as we take it for granted every day, than all the books that were ever written. Yet the names of those who did this work are forgotten. Who invented the wheel, or ships, or the city, or contracts? Who first used a future tense or spoke of conscience or the freedom of the will? These were all matters of evolution if you choose, but not evolved without human effort—and one man or many, the makers of the very framework and tissue of our life are unknown. The triumphs of those even who are illustrious lie outside the little area of their reputation. A great man like Descartes at the beginning of a century puts his finger upon an electric button and at its end, a hundred years later, his thoughts become a force and men who never heard of him begin to move according to his command. In these days when the continuity of human development has become a commonplace one hardly needs to argue that our influence upon those who come after us is not measured by their familiarity with our names. We lawyers may take courage then. We are shaping the future, even if the future undoes all that we do. We shall be recognized, never fear, as well by reaction as by action. Everything tells in its due proportion, in the organic processes of social growth. Nature knows no such thing as a force not counting for its full number of foot-pounds. I say these things because I think one of the best things an older man can do for younger men is to tell them the encouraging thoughts his experience has taught him. It is better still if he can lift up their hearts—if after many battles which were not all victories, the old soldier still feels that fire in him which will impart to them the leaven of his enthusiasm. The flags still flutter and droop—the flowers are hardly faded—where they were placed last Friday over the graves of the dead soldiers who more than a quarter of a century ago were my companions and friends. Every year the procession of worn and gray-haired men who visit their comrades' tombs grows shorter and the escort of their sons who follow them grows longer. In another twenty-five years few indeed will remain of the Grand Army of the Republic. But I believe that the young men who have followed them upon their memorial marches will somehow have caught from that association a spark which will not die out. I would that in like manner we could give to those who follow us in this great procession of life the conviction that while one lives there is neither logic nor joy in living languidly, that there is duty and delight in hard fighting, that while it is well to hit the mark, it is sometimes better to shoot an arrow into the sky if it takes fire there, and that always

> There is no danger to a man that knows
> What life and death is; there's not any law
> Exceeds his knowledge.

THE USE OF COLLEGES

Speech at a Dinner of the Alumni of Yale University, Boston, February 3, 1891

MR. CHAIRMAN AND GENTLEMEN: At every feast it is well to have a skeleton. At every gathering of the elect, the doubting spirit must be allowed to ask his question. In these days all the old assumptions are being retried by the test of actuality, and at a feast in honor of a college, at a gathering of the elect of Yale, the question will arise, What is the use of colleges, after all?

A question not to be answered without reflection, and one which trenches on the doubts sometimes expressed by extremists whether our civilization is a success. We have made famine and pestilence less likely, it is true, and we have multiplied the number of human beings upon the earth; but I own I see no clear advantage in the latter fact; and on the other hand, I doubt whether men generally are as happy as they were in earlier days with all their dangers, and whether the earth has not lost rather than gained in charm.

Nevertheless, we all believe in civilization, and probably most of us believe that colleges are among its fairest flowers. Why? Not surely as collections of schoolmasters teaching others to be schoolmasters, that they may teach yet others, and so *ad infinitum;* not, I venture to think, mainly as teaching the first steps toward practical success in life, but, if practical knowledge is what we mean by useful knowledge, I would rather say as preserving, discovering, and imparting useless knowledge—and thus as the concrete image of what makes man man.

Somebody once said to me, "After all, religion is the only interesting thing," and I think it is true if you take the word a little broadly, and include under it the passionate curiosity as well as the passionate awe which we feel in face of the mystery of the universe. This curiosity is the most human appetite we have. We alone of living beings yearn to get a little nearer and ever a little nearer toward the unseen ocean into which pours the stream of things—toward the reality of the phantasmagoria which dance before our eyes for threescore years and ten.

This endless aerial pursuit is our fate, as truly as to bear offspring or to toil for bread. This passion is as genuine and self-justifying as any other. The satisfaction of it is as truly an end in itself as self-preservation. I do not believe that the justification of science and philosophy is to be found in improved machinery and good conduct. Science and philosophy are themselves necessaries of life. By producing them, civilization sufficiently accounts for itself, if it were not absurd to call the inevitable to account.

Harvard and Yale, as cloisters of philosophy, are keepers of the sacred fire. There are trained the martyrs of the future—the pale acolytes of science. There are gathered those who believe that thoughts are mightier than things. There are the strongholds of ideals more remote and vast than fortune. There is kept alive the faith which sets men to a task of which they shall not see the end, and which perhaps may be unaccomplished when the last of the race shall die. There is believed the idealist's creed, which even skeptics may share, that the world cannot mean less than the farthest-reaching thought, cannot be less worthy of reverence than the loftiest aspiration, of man, who is but a part of it, but a leaf of the unimaginable tree.

It is because I believe that creed that I hope that the two colleges, to both of which I owe a great debt, long may keep the belief of their high import, and long may urge one another in generous rivalry to be and to do all that universities may be and do.

WILLIAM ALLEN

Answer to Resolutions of the Bar,
Greenfield, September 15, 1891

GENTLEMEN OF THE BAR: When I heard the sudden news of our associate's death, my second thought was that the Commonwealth had lost a judge not to be replaced—my first was that I had lost a friend.

The Judges of this Court are thrown so much and so closely together by their work that they are intimate with one another perforce; and to be intimate with William Allen was necessarily to love and admire him. The bar found him very silent upon the bench. He was not so in the consultation room. There he expressed himself freely, and at times, notwithstanding his quiet manner, with the warmth of a hearty and somewhat impulsive temperament, so that there was no question that we knew not only his opinions, but the man behind them.

He seemed to me a typical New Englander, both in character and in ways of thinking; a characteristic product of one of those inland towns which have been our glory—centers large enough to have a society and a culture of their own, and, formerly at least, remote enough to have local traditions, and local rather than cosmopolitan standards and responsibilities. As with others whom I have known that were brought up in similar surroundings, his Yankee caution and sound judgment were leavened with a touch of enthusiasm capable of becoming radical at moments, and his cultivation had destroyed rather than fostered his respect for the old merely as such. He was very kind. He was always perfectly considerate and reasonable, as well as warm of feeling. In ill health as in good he took his share of work without a word or hint of what it cost him until he died. He had the subtlety of a Calvinist theologian, and as sound a training in the common law as was to be found in Massachusetts; but he was saved from becoming over technical by his good sense, his humanitarian turn, and the occasional slight touch of radicalism which I have noted. I never felt quite sure that nothing had been overlooked in a statement of facts, until his eye had scrutinized it. In discussion, if you did not agree with him, you always reached an exact issue, and escape in generalities was impossible. I know few qualities which seem to me more desirable in a judge of a court of last resort than this accuracy of thought, and the habit of keeping one's eye on the things for which words stand. Many men, especially as they grow older, resent attempts to push analysis beyond consecrated phrases, or to formulate anew. Such attempts disturb the intellectual rest for which we long. Our ideal is repose, perhaps because our destiny is effort, just as the eye sees green after gazing at the sun. Judge Allen had none of this weakness, but went on without rest to the end.

William Allen

Great places make great men. The electric current of large affairs turns even common mold to diamond, and traditions of ancient honor impart something of their dignity to those who inherit them. No man of any loftiness of soul could be long a Justice of this Court without rising to his full height. But our dead brother seemed to me too modest to be ambitious for reputation, and to regard his place mainly as an opportunity and a duty. He would have been most pleased, too, I dare say, to slip from it and from life, when his hour came, without remark. He would have preferred not to be celebrated with guns and bells and pealing requiems, the flutter of flags and gleam of steel in the streets, and all the pomp which properly is spent on those who have held power in their right hand. . . . I too am content for him that it should be so, if this neglect of outward show means, even for a chosen few, that their eyes have taken a wider sweep, and have seen that such symbols do not express the vast and shadowy command which a thinker holds. Our prevailing ideals are somewhat coarse. Comparatively few imaginations are educated to aspire beyond money and the immediate forms of power. I have no doubt that vulgar conceptions of life at the top are one of the causes of discontent at the bottom of society. Unless we are to accept decadence as the necessary end of civilization, we should be grateful to all men like William Allen, whose ambition, if it can be called so, looks only to remote and mediated command; who do not ask to say to any one, Go, and he goeth, so long as in truthful imagination they wield, according to their degree, that most subtile and intoxicating authority which controls the future from within by shaping the thoughts and speech of a later time.

Such men are to be honored, not by regiments moving with high heads to martial music, but by a few others, lonely as themselves, walking apart in meditative silence, and dreaming in their turn the dream of spiritual reign.

PAUL BOURGET

Remarks at a Tavern Club Dinner,
December 4, 1893

Mr. Chairman and Gentlemen: I have double reason to thank you for your hospitality in giving me a chance to meet M. Bourget. He is a friend of a very dear friend of mine, whom we all admire—Mr. Henry James—and both before and since I knew of that ground of personal interest, his books have said many things to me which I was very glad to hear. Men are like trees. Without a core which has grown in the past they could not stand—but that core is dead, or at least has ceased to feel, and their life is in the little film of bark where the tissue is just forming. Only those exist for us who nourish that slender film. There are few who take for granted just the things which we demand that they should and who say just what we long to hear. I will remember the feeling of delighted intellectual ease with which I read the *Essais de Psychologie Contemporaine* when they first appeared.

It would be out of place to rehearse at length one's debts to your guest. But one I must venture to mention, already referred to by Mr. Wendell—the Marquis de

Source: M. A. DeWolfe Howe, *Semi-Centennial History of the Tavern Club, 1884–1934* (Boston, 1934), p. 71.

Montjanon in *Cosmopolis.* Who could be more remote from our everyday conceptions that he? In a country where the duel has been given up for a hundred years, only the orthodox or the conceited take themselves seriously. The sentimental optimism of New England thinks of war as all but over—the cynical ideal of commerce is Jay Gould not General Sherman. If, as I suspect, New England is wrong—if possibly commerce is not going to have everything its own way in the future, the types that are bred from war still have value for us. But if not —if, as, externally, idealists usually are, the gentleman and the soldier is a survival, still it is a joy to some of us to see embodied in a lovely picture man's most peculiar power—the power to deny the actual and to perish.

Common sense very often means taking the meaner view. When I feel myself too much mastered by such views, I remember that in my youth I knew some who with different form and color were of the type of M. de Montjanon—and I thank your guest for having enriched my life with this noble portrait.

RUDYARD KIPLING

Remarks at a Tavern Club Dinner, April 24, 1895

MR. CHAIRMAN AND GENTLEMEN: If I were dividing human interests I should put feeling at one pole, and explanation at the other. And therefore I should say that artists on the one side, and philosophers or jurists on the other were as far apart as men could be. But however great the difference, it is difference between men. We are all human, and even a lawyer may lay his wreath of dry leaves at Mr. Kipling's feet. I leave it to others to do justice to him as an artist, as a born story teller who has rediscovered the careless confidence of touch of the great masters. But I will say a word on a more universal aspect in which his work has presented itself to me. In talking with one or two laboring men more or less prominent as leaders in their efforts for change I have said to them several times, "I see that you and your people have *aims*, but I don't see that you have *ideals*. Have you read Mr. Kipling's Stories? Mulvaney and Ortheris, although they would not have known what the word meant, had ideals. Mulvaney and Ortheris did believe, and to read about them makes others believe, that there is something in the

SOURCE: M. A. DeWolfe Howe, *Semi-Centennial History of the Tavern Club, 1884–1934* (Boston, 1934), p. 73.

world besides comfort, something worth loving and worth dying for." Mr. Kipling has written war songs. He has lifted up our hearts and made it easier to be valiant.

In literature I think there are three stages. There is the stage of primitive innocence. There is the stage of knowing negations, when *chic* is the superlative of excellence and Mephistopheles is God. And there is at last something on the other side of *chic*, where greatness begins.

It is better to be knowing than to be innocent, but it is better still to have reached that upper ether where the lightning of Judic's or Gyp's blasting wink cannot reach. Unless I am mistaken, it is in that upper ether that our guest belongs.

THE SOLDIER'S FAITH

An Address Delivered on Memorial Day, May 30, 1895, At a Meeting Called by the Graduating Class of Harvard University

Any day in Washington Street, when the throng is greatest and busiest, you may see a blind man playing a flute. I suppose that some one hears him. Perhaps also my pipe may reach the heart of some passer in the crowd.

I once heard a man say, "Where Vanderbilt sits, there is the head of the table. I teach my son to be rich." He said what many think. For although the generation born about 1840, and now governing the world, has fought two at least of the greatest wars in history, and has witnessed others, war is out of fashion, and the man who commands the attention of his fellows is the man of wealth. Commerce is the great power. The aspirations of the world are those of commerce. Moralists and philosophers, following its lead, declare that war is wicked, foolish, and soon to disappear.

The society for which many philanthropists, labor reformers, and men of fashion unite in longing is one in which they may be comfortable and may shine without much trouble or any danger. The unfortunately growing hatred of the poor for the rich seems to me to rest on the belief that money is the main thing (a belief in which the poor have been encouraged by the rich), more than on any grievance. Most of my hearers would rather that their daughters or their sisters should marry a son of one of the great rich families than a regular army officer, were he as beautiful, brave, and gifted as Sir William Napier. I have heard the question asked whether our war was worth fighting, after all. There are many, poor and rich, who think that love of country is an old wife's tale, to be replaced by interest in a labor union, or, under the name of cosmopolitanism, by a rootless self-seeking search for a place where the most enjoyment may be had at the least cost.

Meantime we have learned the doctrine that evil means pain, and the revolt against pain in all its forms has grown more and more marked. From societies for the prevention of cruelty to animals up to socialism, we express in numberless ways the notion that suffering is a wrong which can be and ought to be prevented, and a whole literature of sympathy has sprung into being which points out in story and in verse how hard it is to be wounded in the battle of life, how terrible, how unjust it is that any one should fail.

Even science has had its part in the tendencies which we observe. It has shaken established religion in the minds of very many. It has pursued analysis until at last this thrilling world of colors and sounds and passions has seemed fatally to resolve itself into one vast network of vibrations endlessly weaving an aimless web, and the rainbow flush of cathedral windows, which once to enraptured eyes appeared the very smile of God, fades slowly out into the pale irony of the void.

And yet from vast orchestras still comes the music of mighty symphonies. Our painters even now are spreading along the walls of our Library glowing symbols of mysteries still real, and the hardly silenced cannon of the East proclaim once more that combat and pain still are the portion of man. For my own part, I believe that the struggle for life is the order of the world, at which it is vain to repine. I can imagine the burden changed in the way in which it is to be borne, but I cannot imagine that it ever will be lifted from men's backs. I can imagine a future in which science shall have passed from the combative to the dogmatic stage, and shall have gained such catholic acceptance that it shall take control of life, and condemn at once with instant execution what now is left for nature to destroy. But we are far from such a future, and we cannot stop to amuse or to terrify ourselves with dreams. Now, at least, and perhaps as long as man dwells upon the globe, his destiny is battle, and he has to take the chances of war. If it is our business to fight, the book for the army is a war-song, not a hospital-sketch. It is not well for soldiers to think much about wounds. Sooner or later we shall fall; but meantime it is for us to fix our eyes upon the point to be stormed, and to get there if we can.

Behind every scheme to make the world over, lies the question, What kind of a world do you want? The ideals of the past for men have been drawn from war, as those for women have been drawn from motherhood. For all our prophecies, I doubt if we are ready to give up our inheritance. Who is there who would not like to be thought a gentleman? Yet what has that name been built on but the soldier's choice of honor rather than life? To be a soldier or descended from soldiers, in time of peace to be ready to give one's life rather than to suffer disgrace, that is what the word has meant; and if we try to claim it at less cost than a splendid carelessness for life, we are trying to steal the good will without the responsibilities of the place. We will not dispute about tastes. The man of the future may want something different. But who of us could endue a world, although cut up into five-acre lots and having no man upon it who was not well fed and well housed, without the divine folly of honor, without the senseless passion for knowledge out-reaching the flaming bounds of the possible, without ideals the essence of which is that they never can be achieved? I do not know what is true. I do not know the meaning of the universe. But in the midst of doubt, in the collapse of creeds, there is one thing I do not doubt, that no man who lives in the same world with most of us can doubt, and that is that the faith is true and adorable which leads a soldier to throw away his life in obedience to a blindly accepted duty, in a cause which he little understands, in a plan of campaign of which he has no notion, under tactics of which he does not see the use.

Most men who know battle know the cynic force with which the thoughts of common sense will assail them in times of stress; but they know that in their greatest moments faith has trampled those thoughts under foot. If you have been in line, suppose on Tremont Street Mall, ordered simply to wait and to do nothing, and have watched the enemy bring their guns to bear upon you down a gentle slope like that from Beacon Street, have seen the puff of the firing, have felt the burst of the spherical case-shot as it came toward you, have heard and seen the shrieking fragments go tearing through your company, and have known that the next or the next shot carries your fate; if you have advanced in line and have seen ahead of you the spot which you must pass where the rifle bullets are striking; if you have ridden by night at a walk toward the blue line of fire at the dead angle of Spottsylvania, where for twenty-four hours the soldiers were fighting on the two sides of an earthwork, and in the morning the dead and dying lay piled in a row six deep, and as you rode have heard the bullets splashing in the mud and earth about you; if you have been on the picket-line at night in a black and unknown wood, have heard the spat of the bullets upon the trees, and as you moved have felt your foot slip upon a dead man's body; if you have had a blind fierce gallop against the enemy, with your blood up and a pace that left no time for fear —if, in short, as some, I hope many, who hear me, have known, you have known the vicissitudes of terror and of triumph in war, you know that there is such a thing as the faith I spoke of. You know your own weakness and are modest; but you know that man has in him that unspeakable somewhat which makes him capable of miracle, able to lift himself by the might of his own soul, unaided, able to face annihilation for a blind belief.

From the beginning, to us, children of the North, life has seemed a place hung about by dark mists, out of which come the pale shine of dragon's scales, and the cry of fighting men, and the sound of swords. Beowulf, Milton, Dürer, Rembrandt, Schopenhauer, Turner, Tennyson, from the first war-song of our race to the stall-fed poetry of modern English drawing-rooms, all have had the same vision, and all have had a glimpse of a light to be followed. "The end of worldly life awaits us all. Let him who may, gain honor ere death. That is best for a warrior when he is dead." So spoke Beowulf a thousand years ago.

> Not of the sunlight,
> Not of the moonlight,
> Not of the starlight!
> O young Mariner,
> Down to the haven,
> Call your companions,
> Launch your vessel,
> And crowd your canvas,
> And, ere it vanishes
> Over the margin,
> After it, follow it,
> Follow The Gleam.

So sang Tennyson in the voice of the dying Merlin.

When I went to the war I thought that soldiers were old men. I remembered a picture of the revolutionary soldier which some of you may have seen, representing a white-haired man with his flint-lock slung across his back. I remembered one or two living examples of revolutionary soldiers whom I had met, and I took no account of the lapse of time. It was not until long after, in winter quarters, as I was listening to some of the sentimental songs in vogue, such as—

> Farewell, Mother, you may never
> See your darling boy again,

that it came over me that the army was made up of what I now should call very young men. I dare say that my illusion has been shared by some of those now present, as they have looked at us upon whose heads the white shadows have begun to fall. But the truth is that war is the business of youth and early middle age. You who called this assemblage together, not we, would be the soldiers of another war, if we should have one, and we speak to you as the dying Merlin did in the verse which I just quoted. Would that the blind man's pipe might be transfigured by Merlin's magic, to make you hear the bugles as once we heard them beneath the morning stars! For you it is that now is sung the Song of thc Sword:

> The War-Thing, the Comrade,
> Father of honor
> And giver of kingship,
> The fame-smith, the song master.
>
> . . . .
>
> *Priest* (saith the Lord)
> *Of his marriage with victory.*
>
> . . . .

Clear singing, clean slicing;
Sweet spoken, soft finishing;
Making death beautiful,
Life but a coin
To be staked in the pastime
Whose playing is more
Than the transfer of being;
Arch-anarch, chief builder,
Prince and evangelist,
I am the Will of God:
I am the Sword.

War, when you are at it, is horrible and dull. It is only when time has passed that you see that its message was divine. I hope it may be long before we are called again to sit at that master's feet. But some teacher of the kind we all need. In this snug, over-safe corner of the world we need it, that we may realize that our comfortable routine is no eternal necessity of things, but merely a little space of calm in the midst of the tempestuous untamed streaming of the world, and in order that we may be ready for danger. We need it in this time of individualist negations, with its literature of French and American humor, revolting at discipline, loving flesh-pots, and denying that anything is worthy of reverence—in order that we may remember all that buffoons forget. We need it everywhere and at all times. For high and dangerous action teaches us to believe as right beyond dispute things for which our doubting minds are slow to find words of proof. Out of heroism grows faith in the worth of heroism. The proof comes later, and even may never come. Therefore I rejoice at every dangerous sport which I see pursued. The students at

Heidelberg, with their sword-slashed faces, inspire me with sincere respect. I gaze with delight upon our polo-players. If once in a while in our rough riding a neck is broken, I regard it, not as a waste, but as a price well paid for the breeding of a race fit for headship and command.

We do not save our traditions, in this country. The regiments whose battle-flags were not large enough to hold the names of the battles they had fought, vanished with the surrender of Lee, although their memories inherited would have made heroes for a century. It is the more necessary to learn the lesson afresh from perils newly sought, and perhaps it is not vain for us to tell the new generation what we learned in our day, and what we still believe. That the joy of life is living, is to put out all one's powers as far as they will go; that the measure of power is obstacles overcome; to ride boldly at what is in front of you, be it fence or enemy; to pray, not for comfort, but for combat; to keep the soldier's faith against the doubts of civil life, more besetting and harder to overcome than all the misgivings of the battle-field, and to remember that duty is not to be proved in the evil day, but then to be obeyed unquestioning; to love glory more than the temptations of wallowing ease, but to know that one's final judge and only rival is oneself: with all our failures in act and thought, these things we learned from noble enemies in Virginia or Georgia or on the Mississippi, thirty years ago; these things we believe to be true.

> "Life is not lost," she said, "for which is bought
> Endlesse renowm."

We learned also, and we still believe, that love of country is not yet an idle name.

> Deare countrey! O how dearely deare
> Ought thy remembraunce, and perpetuall band
> Be to thy foster-child, that from thy hand
> Did common breath and nouriture receave!
> How brutish is it not to understand
> How much to her we owe, that all us gave;
> That gave unto us all, whatever good we have!

As for us, our days of combat are over. Our swords are rust. Our guns will thunder no more. The vultures that once wheeled over our heads are buried with their prey. Whatever of glory yet remains for us to win must be won in the council or the closet, never again in the field. I do not repine. We have shared the incommunicable experience of war; we have felt, we still feel, the passion of life to its top.

Three years ago died the old colonel of my regiment, the Twentieth Massachusetts. He gave our regiment its soul. No man could falter who heard his "Forward, Twentieth!" I went to his funeral. From a side door of the church a body of little choir-boys came in like a flight of careless doves. At the same time the doors opened at the front, and up the main aisle advanced his coffin, followed by the few gray heads who stood for the men of the Twentieth, the rank and file whom he had loved, and whom he led for the last time. The church was empty. No one remembered the old man whom we were burying, no one save those next to him, and us. And I said to myself, The Twentieth has shrunk to a skeleton, a ghost, a memory, a forgotten name which we other old men alone keep in our hearts. And then I thought: It is right. It is as the colonel would have had it. This also is part of the soldier's faith: Having known great things, to be content with silence. Just then there fell into my hands a little song sung by a warlike people on the Danube, which seemed to me fit for a soldier's last word, another song of the sword, but a song of the sword in its scabbard, a song of oblivion and peace.

A soldier has been buried on the battle-field.

> And when the wind in the tree-tops roared,
> The soldier asked from the deep dark grave:
> "Did the banner flutter then?"
> "Not so, my hero," the wind replied,
> "The fight is done, but the banner won,
> Thy comrades of old have borne it hence,
> Have borne it in triumph hence."
> Then the soldier spake from the deep dark grave:
> "I am content."
>
> . . . .
>
> Then he heareth the lovers laughing pass,
> And the soldier asks once more:
> "Are these not the voices of them that love,
> That love—and remember me?"
> "Not so, my hero," the lovers say,
> "We are those that remember not;
> For the spring has come and the earth has smiled,
> And the dead must be forgot."
> Then the soldier spake from the deep dark grave:
> "I am content."

LEARNING AND SCIENCE

Speech at a Dinner of the Harvard Law School Association in Honor of Professor C. C. Langdell, June 25, 1895

Mr. President and Gentlemen of the Association: As most of those here have graduated from the Law School within the last twenty-five years, I know that I am in the presence of very learned men. For my own part, lately my thoughts have been turned to

> old, unhappy, far-off things,
> And battles long ago;

and when once the ghosts of the dead fifers of thirty years since begin to play in my head, the laws are silent. And yet as I look around me, I think to myself, like Correggio, "I too am, or at least have been, a pedagogue." And as such I will venture a reflection.

Learning, my learned brethren, is a very good thing. I should be the last to undervalue it, having done my share of quotation from the Year Books. But it is liable to lead us astray. The law, so far as it depends on learning, is indeed, as it has been called, the government of the living by the dead. To a very considerable extent no doubt it is inevitable that the living should be so governed.

The past gives us our vocabulary and fixes the limits of our imagination; we cannot get away from it. There is, too, a peculiar logical pleasure in making manifest the continuity between what we are doing and what has been done before. But the present has a right to govern itself so far as it can; and it ought always to be remembered that historic continuity with the past is not a duty, it is only a necessity.

I hope that the time is coming when this thought will bear fruit. An ideal system of law should draw its postulates and its legislative justification from science. As it is now, we rely upon tradition, or vague sentiment, or the fact that we never thought of any other way of doing things, as our only warrant for rules which we enforce with as much confidence as if they embodied revealed wisdom. Who here can give reasons of any different kind for believing that half the criminal law does not do more harm than good? Our forms of contract, instead of being made once for all, like a yacht, on lines of least resistance, are accidental relics of early notions, concerning which the learned dispute. How much has reason had to do in deciding how far, if at all, it is expedient for the State to meddle with the domestic relations? And so I might go on through the whole law.

The Italians have begun to work upon the notion that the foundations of the law ought to be scientific, and, if our civilization does not collapse, I feel pretty sure that the regiment or division that follows us will carry that flag. Our own word seems the last always; yet the change of emphasis from an argument in Plowden to one in the time of Lord Ellenborough, or even from that to one in our own day, is as marked as the difference between Cowley's poetry and Shelley's. Other changes as great will happen. And so the eternal procession moves on, we in the front for the moment; and, stretching away against the unattainable sky, the black spearheads of the army that has been passing in unbroken line already for near a thousand years.

ARTHUR P. BONNEY AND FREDERIC T. GREENHALGE

Answer to Resolutions of the Bar, Lowell, April 21, 1896

GENTLEMEN OF THE BAR: You bid me join you in commemorating two of our brethren, each of more than common mark, and each dying in a glory of his own, one at the head of the state, the other in "the monumental pomp of age," after a career of great success. I have relied on you to tell their stories and to estimate their work, for you were nearer to them and I was far off and my words could do no more than faintly echo yours. Mr. Bonney I never saw but once. The Governor since he left the law for politics I have met only on state occasions. At an earlier date I did meet him. The first jury case over which I presided as a judge was tried in this room and Mr. Greenhalge was one of the counsel. I well remember how the anxiety with which I began

SOURCE: *Memorials of Arthur P. Bonney and Frederic T. Greenhalge Presented to the Supreme Judicial Court, April 21, 1896* (Lowell, 1896).

Arthur P. Bonney (1828–1896) was among the leaders of the bar of Middlesex County and active in the business and industrial life of Lowell. Frederic T. Greenhalge (1842–1896) was for many years a prominent lawyer and citizen in Lowell. He had served his community as a member of Congress and was thrice elected Republican Governor of Massachusetts, the office which he held at the time of his death.

that new experience turned to pleasure as I found I was dealing with a man to whom it was not necessary to give up candor or manners in order to fight hard and prevail. After that I heard him in court repeatedly, and once or twice I had the pleasure of seeing him at home. The more I saw of him the warmer was my regard, and it seemed to me that the chance to know him was all that was needed to ensure him strong affection. I lament his loss with personal sorrow.

But for most of us the fountain of tears is early dried. One after another we see our brothers go down, and death becomes an ever present companion of our thoughts. The skeleton is always in the corner mumming his silent part, until at last I have come to believe that he is necessary to make the scene complete. Without despair there is no triumph: without death the poignancy departs from life.

For these two I do not see why we should lament, save for our own and the public loss. Each of them died in the full tide of success, one at the natural end of his life, the other when he had found his vocation and shown his courage, his intellect, and his truth. What more can any man ask? The meaning of effort we may not know, the worth to the great world-stream of conscious striving we may not understand. But we know that to strive with all his heart is the destiny of man; we have faith that it has its meaning in the wide welter of the unknown, and when a man has achieved nobly we know that what to us, at least, must be an object of the universe is attained. I leave it there and do not seek as Milton put it, "To justify the ways of God to man."

The death of Mr. Bonney brings home to me as other recent deaths have done, that the law has changed hands since I came to the Bar, and even since I first sat in this court room. Another generation is upon the Bench. Another generation is in the first line at the Bar. We who yesterday were not engaged, and watched, as we held our places in reserve, the dark electric outline of those in front against the white smoke of the firing, have seen their line thin and one by one the leaders drop from their horses. We have had our orders and we have stepped forward to take our turn in the encounter which has but one end. In the short burial truce we carry to the grave our dead with honor and with the contained sorrow of men who know that their own turn is not far off. We say over them the soldier's text: "The good is one thing, the pleasant is another; the wise prefer the good," and we turn back to the front with flags flying and music no longer sad, hiding regret in our hearts, resolved like them "to withstand in the evil day, and having done all, to stand."

The court will now adjourn.

RUDOLPH C. LEHMANN

Remarks at a Tavern Club Dinner, November 24, 1896

I ONCE spent a summer at Niagara Falls and on the fourth of July I went down to see a man go through the rapids on a boat of his construction. I got there a little late and the man was drowned before I arrived. Afterwards a lady talking of the accident said that if the attempt had promised any possible good to his fellow men the case would have been different, but that under the circumstances she could not see any justification for a pure waste of life. I replied, Madam, on the contrary precisely because it was not useful it was a perfect expression of this male contribution to our common stock of morality. Woman, who is the mother, contributes living for another—the ideal of unselfishness. Man who is the breadwinner and the fighter, contributes what boys used to call doing a stump. Perhaps the application was a paradox but the thought is true. An ideal is a principle of conduct carried to its abstract,

SOURCE: M. A. DeWolfe Howe, *Semi-Centennial History of the Tavern Club, 1884–1934* (Boston, 1934), p. 74.

Rudolph Chambers Lehmann (1886–1929), barrister, journalist, and sportsman, was the brother of Lady Nina Campbell, one of Holmes's earliest English friends.

absolute, and therefore useless expression, and when you find such an expression in life it has the final charm. Why do we send expeditions to the North Pole? It is nothing but nations doing stumps to one another. America gets to a certain latitude and then England or some other country says "I think I can get a little higher," and tries; and if she succeeds she has a superlative and double satisfaction, the prides of victory and that of having done a feat which is useless—which is purely ideal—like the Cambridge don who invented an ingenious mathematical theorem and said the best thing about it is that no one can make any use of it for anything. You see where I am coming out. What is a boat race? What difference does it make that one crew can row three miles ten seconds quicker than another? In the immediate—in the coarse and directly practical sense it makes no difference at all. Yet who is there with soul so dead that he does not care more for it than for most useful things—that he would not take a lifelong pride in helping to win one—or to make a worthy contest? This uselessness is the highest kind of use. It is kindling and feeding the ideal spark without which life is not worth living. There are other reasons of which I will not speak which make me glad to welcome our guest here tonight. But this one I may mention in all seriousness as sufficient, that he is here generously to fan that spark and to help to keep alive the old tradition which tells men that to be enduring and disciplined and brave is not less an end of life than to shine in the stock market and to be rich.

GEORGE OTIS SHATTUCK

Answer to Resolutions of the Bar,
Boston, May 29, 1897

GENTLEMEN OF THE BAR: I owe Mr. Shattuck more than I ever have owed any one else in the world, outside my immediate family. From the time when I was a student in his office until he died, he was my dear and intimate friend. He taught me unrepeatable lessons. He did me unnumbered kindnesses. To live while still young in daily contact with his sweeping, all-compelling force, his might of temperament, his swiftness (rarely found with such might), his insight, tact, and subtlety, was to receive an imprint never to be effaced. My education would have been but a thin and poor thing had I missed that great experience. The things he did for me in other practical ways even gratitude cannot enumerate or remember. It seemed to me that he could not find any one near him without interesting himself in his fortunes and his fate.

You cannot expect, then, from me a critical analysis and estimate. I could not sit coldly down to measure and weigh his qualities, or "peep and botanize" upon his grave. He was my dear and honored friend. I can do little more than repeat that.

Some of his qualities, however, were manifest to any one who knew him well. He needed the excitement of advocacy or of some practical end to awaken his insight, but when it was awakened there was no depth of speculation or research which he was not ready and more than able to sound. His work may not always have had the neatness of smaller minds, but it brought out deeply hidden truths by some invisible radiance that searched things to their bones.

He seemed to like to take great burdens upon himself —not merely when there was a corresponding reward, but when his feelings were touched, as well. He was a model in his bearing with clients. How often have I seen men come to him borne down by troubles which they found too great to support, and depart with light step, having left their weight upon stronger shoulders. But while his calm manner made such things seem trifles, he took them a good deal on his nerves. I saw the ends of his fingers twitch as he quietly listened and advised. He never shunned anxiety, and anxiety is what kills.

His swiftness and tact, which I have mentioned, made him great in cross-examination, the command of which the late Mr. Durant used to call the highest gift of a lawyer. A large part of the cross-examination which I hear, even from able men, seems to me to waste time and often to hurt their case. Mr. Shattuck, while he was in the habit of trying cases, rarely made a mistake. He saw the bearing of every answer on every part of the evidence. If by any chance he got an unexpected reply, he adjusted himself to it in a flash, and met it by a new approach from some remote side. He could bring out the prejudices that unfitted a witness for just this case, and yet leave his general value and his personal feelings untouched, with a delicacy, clearness, and force that left me simply astounded.

At the time to which I refer, when I first knew him, and while he still tried many cases, he was a great man with the jury in every way. His addresses carried everything before them like a victorious cavalry charge, sometimes, as it seemed to me, sweeping the judge along with the rest in the rout. Latterly his most successful appearances were in arguments of law. He had learned the all too rarely learned lesson of pointed brevity. In a few luminous words he went to the bottom of his question, and then took his seat. In short, I know of no form of forensic effort in which at some time in his career he had not reached as high a point as I personally ever have seen attained.

He was no less eminent in his work out of court. He was one of the wisest and most far-seeing of advisers. I know of splendidly victorious men who have said that but for his help when the battle was turning against them they would have gone down in the fight.

But that great vitality found only a partial outlet and expression in the law. He liked to ride and drive and sail and farm, and at times to talk. His fondness for farming was a noticeable feature. I think he had a sympathy with the great, quiet forces which he saw at work, and a sympathy with the animals of the farm. Also the visible return which the earth makes for labor pleased him.

It made him realize that he was adding to the world's stores.

I have had much delight in his companionship. Whether driving over the sandy roads of the Cape, or sailing in his yacht, or dining at his house, or at some later and less regular entertainment in the garret in which I used to live, he had a kind of benevolent beaming in his face and heart which gave unction to enjoyment.

People often speak of correcting the judgment of the time by that of posterity. I think it is quite as true to say that we must correct the judgment of posterity by that of the time. A small man may be remembered for some little felicity which enabled him to write a successful lyric, or in some way to charm the senses or emotions of a world always readier with its rewards for pleasures than for great thoughts or deeds. But I know of no true measure of men except the total of human energy which they embody—counting everything, with due allowance for quality, from Nansen's power to digest blubber or to resist cold, up to his courage, or to Wordsworth's power to express the unutterable, or to Kant's speculative reach. The final test of this energy is battle in some form—actual war—the crush of Arctic ice—the fight for mastery in the market or the court. Many of those who are remembered have spared themselves this supreme trial, and have fostered a faculty at the expense of their total life. It is one thing to utter a happy phrase from a protected cloister; another to think under fire—to think for action upon which great interests depend. The most powerful men are apt to go into the mêlée and fall or come out generals. The great problems are questions of here and now. Questions of here and now occupy nine hundred and ninety-nine thousandths of the ability of the world; and when the now has passed and has given place to another now, the heads and hands that built the organic structure of society are forgotten from the speech of their fellows, and live only in the tissue of their work.

Such may be the fate of the man whom to-day we remember and honor. But remembered or forgotten, few indeed, I believe, of those whom I have seen have counted for as much in the hardest work of the day. I do not regret that it should be known by few. What is any remembrance of men to our high ambition? Sooner or later the race of men will die; but we demand an eternal record. We have it. What we have done is woven forever into the great vibrating web of the world. The eye that can read the import of its motion can decipher the story of all our deeds, of all our thoughts. To that eye I am content to leave the recognition and the memory of this great head and heart.

COMMENCEMENT ADDRESS

Brown University, June 17, 1897

A UNIVERSITY is a place from which men start for the Eternal City. In the university are pictured the ideals which abide in the City of God. Many roads lead to that haven, and those who are here have traveled by different paths towards the goal. I do not know what better the travelers can do at a gathering like this, where for a moment the university becomes conscious of itself and of its meaning, than to report to those about to start something of their experiences and to give a hint of what is to be expected on the way.

My way has been by ocean of the Law. On that I have learned a part of the great lesson, the lesson not of law but of life. There were few of the charts and lights for which one longed when I began. One found oneself plunged in a thick fog of details—in a black and frozen night, in which were no flowers, no spring, no easy joys. Voices of authority warned that in the crush of that ice any craft might sink. One heard Burke saying that law sharpens the mind by narrowing it. One heard in

SOURCE: *Collected Legal Papers* (New York, 1920), p. 164. A manuscript copy, in Holmes's hand, is among the Holmes papers at the Harvard Law School. The address is reprinted here with the permission of the copyright owner, Harcourt, Brace & Company.

Thackeray of a lawyer bending all the powers of a great mind to a mean profession. One saw that artists and poets shrank from it as from an alien world. One doubted oneself how it could be worthy of the interest of an intelligent mind. And yet one said to oneself, Law is human—it is part of man, and of one world with all the rest. There must be a drift, if one will go prepared and have patience, which will bring one out to daylight and a worthy end. You all have read or heard the story of Nansen and see the parallel which I use. Most men of the college-bred type in some form or other have to go through that experience of sailing for the ice and letting themselves be frozen in. In the first stage one has companions, cold and black though it be, and if he sticks to it, he finds at last that there is a drift as was foretold. When he has found that he has learned the first part of his lesson, that one is safe in trusting to courage and to time. But he has not yet learned all. So far his trials have been those of his companions. But if he is a man of high ambitions he must leave even his fellow-adventurers and go forth into a deeper solitude and greater trials. He must start for the pole. In plain words he must face the loneliness of original work. No one can cut out new paths in company. He does that alone.

When he has done that and has turned misgivings into success he is master of himself and knows the secret of achievement. He has learned the second part of his lesson and is ready for the consummation of the whole. For he has gained another knowledge more fruitful than success. He knows now what he had divined at the outset, that one part of the universe yields the same teaching as any other if only it is mastered, that the difference between the great way of taking things and the small—between philosophy and gossip—is only the difference between realizing the part as a part of a whole and looking at it in its isolation as if it really stood apart. The consummation to which I referred comes when he applies this knowledge to himself. He may put it in the theological form of justification by faith or in the philosophical one of the continuity of the universe. I care not very much for the form if in some way he has learned that he cannot set himself over against the universe as a rival god, to criticize it, or to shake his fist at the skies, but that his meaning is its meaning, his only worth is as a part of it, as a humble instrument of the universal power. It seems to me that this is the key to intellectual salvation, as the key to happiness is to accept a like faith in one's heart, and to be not merely a necessary but a willing instrument in working out the inscrutable end.

THE FRATERNITY OF ARMS

Remarks at a Meeting
of the 20th Regimental Association,
December 11, 1897

FELLOW SOLDIERS OF THE 20TH: I made no preparations for a set speech to you. It would not be natural if I did. We have heard each other cursing as we stumbled through the long night marches—we have worked together in dreadful silence through the summer dust when we could only see the bayonet of the man ahead—we have stood side by side in line—we have charged and swept the enemy—and we have run away like rabbits—all together. And when men have seen each other inside out it is too late for one of them to stand up and make orations to the rest. As I once heard a man say: You can't fool your own brother. So all that I shall say is that I am glad to see you once more. Time has passed since those days, the memory of which brings us together. We are getting to be old fellows and already feel rather complimented still to be called middle-aged men. When I look at it one way it seems to me to have passed as you see a juggler twitch off a table cloth and have every-

SOURCE: a manuscript copy, in Holmes's hand, preserved among the Holmes papers at the Harvard Law School.

thing that was on it standing just as before. But things have not stood still. The list of ghosts grows long. The roster of men grows short. My memory of those stirring days has faded to a blurred dream. Only one thing has not changed. As I look into your eyes I feel as I always do that a great trial in your youth made you different—made all of us different from what we could have been without it. It made us feel the brotherhood of man. It made us citizens of the world and not of a little town. And best of all it made us believe in something else besides doing the best for ourselves and getting all the loaves and fishes we could. I hate to hear old soldiers telling what heroes they were. We did just what any other Americans—what the last generation would have done, what the next generation would if put in our place. But we had the good luck to learn a lesson early which has given a different feeling to life. We learned to believe that doing one's duty is better than the loaves and fishes and that honor is better than a whole skin. To know that, puts a kind of fire into a man's heart, and there is nowhere a man learns it as he does in battle. Those who died there died, as a soldier said hundreds of years ago, with a bird singing in their breast. Those of us who survive have heard the same music and through all the hard work of later years have remembered that once we listened to strains from a higher world.

EDWARD AVERY AND ERASTUS WORTHINGTON

Answer to Resolutions of the Bar, Dedham, May 2, 1898

GENTLEMEN OF THE BAR: One of the early experiences which I had of the great billows of the open sea after leaving the quiet harbor of another lawyer's office was an encounter with Mr. Avery. It was an instructive experience, and I always shall remember him as one of the really very able lawyers whom I have met—an intellect which was subtle and profound as life, which did not run in grooves determined by some previous case or preconceived idea but struck deep into the facts as they were. A large part of what are called able arguments follow conventional lines and run in channels more or less prepared. It is an exceptional mind that is only fortified and is not trammeled by knowledge and that thinks *things* not words—that is to say, that realizes even par-

SOURCE: a manuscript copy, in Holmes's hand, preserved among the Holmes papers at the Harvard Law School.

Edward Avery (1828–1896) was one of the leaders of Suffolk bar, noted for his skill in jury trials, and a prominent figure in the Democratic Party. Erastus Worthington (1828–1898) for thirty years was Clerk of Courts for Norfolk County. Like his father before him, he was a local historian of extensive learning and wrote a useful history of the bench and bar of Norfolk County.

tially the facts of life of which words are only symbols. The best of us do it imperfectly, and most of us simply carry on the traditions in which we have been brought up, as mechanically as a plant grows. It is an exceptional mind, too, that gives you only its personal reaction and has the reserve and the intelligence to take what the past has made commonplace for granted. If I divine rightly from what little I saw of Mr. Avery in the way of his profession and also in a few chance but singularly agreeable conversations, he had one of the most living intelligences that I have known at the bar. I may add that I am struck by the strong personal liking and kind feeling that I have heard expressed for him by members of the bar who knew him well, as I did not, both at this meeting and before.

Mr. Worthington was the Clerk of this Court for the greater part of the fifteen years and more that I have been upon the bench. Yet the accidents of affairs were such that I hardly more than met him during all that time. Once when I was at the bar I had a glimpse of him as a dangerous antagonist, but it was only a glimpse. So that the personal impressions which I have about him are few and personal impressions and judgments are the only things that justify speech. I believed him to be a superior man. I knew his zealous energy. I realized that his was not one of those half obliterated personalities of which we have too many. When I think of the future of my country I do not worry about her institutions if only I can feel sure that it will produce a well-nourished race—a race of courageous self-willed men who on occasion are capable of being fierce. Mr. Worthington, little as I knew him, was one of those who gave me hope for the future because he showed that we still can produce from an old Yankee strain an adequate type—full-blooded, honest, brave, intent as a man should be on making his will prevail, while always setting his will to ends which in his soul he believed right.

It is pleasant to think that both Mr. Avery and Mr. Worthington have left behind them successors who inherit the good will and kind feeling of the bar for their fathers—a good will and kind feeling that cannot be bequeathed unless they are earned.

Brethren—we pass from the Abyss *I know not whence* into the Abyss *I know not whither*, and as each of us in his turn leaves the light some one who loved him utters a cry and then the great silence prevails once more. The Churches wisely have prepared for those supreme events which are common to us all liturgies which deal with the universal in universal terms. There is no such service at our command. Neither have we the funeral march and the fire of guns with which the army commits its dead soldiers to the grave. We are here—a few men in a room, unhelped, simply stopping for a moment to look the greatest of all facts in the face, to honor the dead, and then like soldiers to go back to the front and fight until we follow our brothers. Both of those whom we commemorate were fighting men and so helped to teach us how to do our fighting—helped us to remember that when war has begun any cause is good, that life is war, and that the part of man in it is to be strong. We shall not soon forget them, and we shall try to do our part.

The resolutions which you offer will be entered on the records of the Court.

The Court will now adjourn.

ALBERT VENN DICEY

Remarks at a Tavern Club Dinner, November 4, 1898

MORE THAN thirty years ago there came to this country two young Englishmen of whom England has heard a good deal since that time. One was Mr. James Bryce, whose name at least we all know so well. The other the guest in whose honor we are met tonight. At that time I began with both of them a friendship which has continued warm and sincere to the present day. It is delightful to me therefore that this club should offer its hospitality to my distinguished friend. It delights me as a not very often recurring compensation, that a society so largely devoted to the arts should once in a while pay to the law a tribute which it more frequently exacts from the law in favor of the arts.

Nothing strikes me more in life—nothing strikes me more in clubs made up of men of different callings—than the almost willful inarticulateness of one to another among men of different pursuits. If I may venture to say so this exclusiveness is peculiarly marked in artists. The painter, the musician, or the poet has nothing to say to

SOURCE: a manuscript copy, in Holmes's hand, preserved among the Holmes papers at the Harvard Law School.

the man of business or the lawyer and the compliment sometimes is returned. One man thinks that his interest is beauty or harmony or uttering the unutterable and another that his is money or law or abstract truth, and both believe that there is a gulf between them. Yet really the interest of all men is the same. The interest of men is not money or beauty or truth but the pursuit of money or beauty or truth. And all experience the same vital pleasure—the one great pleasure and end of life—that of realizing their own spontaneous energy through whatever channel they are able to bring it out. More than that. So far as there is an intellectual element in their activity at all, the foundation of greatness, that which is behind all manifestations of power, and compared with which imagination, that much overworked word, is superficial, is one and the same: Insight. It may be insight into the determining features of a landscape—it may be insight into the great lines of human history—it may be insight into the reaction between a mass of economic facts and the imaginations of men—it may be insight into the character of individual man, but always insight at bottom one and the same supreme gift.

Therefore men who have shown themselves distinguished for this gift in some of its directions naturally and properly do honor to one who has shown it preëminently in another, not as strangers but as brothers.

I do not want to praise my friend Dicey too highly because there are a few small points upon which we differ and in which of course he is wrong. But he has produced noble works full of the quality of which I have spoken and has produced them in a new form which he more than anyone else has brought into vogue among modern writers upon the law.

Harvard University is to be congratulated for having had his instruction—the people of Boston for having the opportunity of listening to the more general views suggested by his studies—and this club for our personal meeting with one of the pleasantest men and most brilliant talkers whom I have ever met.

ADMIRAL DEWEY

Speech Prepared for Delivery at a Banquet, October 14, 1899

THE WHOLE country has risen up to do unprecedented honor—to whom and to what? To a fighting man and to an astonishing victory. We have not yet outgrown armies and navies and at this moment we all do them the honor they deserve. Who can feel it more than a representative of the law? For the law does not mean sympathetic advice which you may neglect if you choose, but stern monition that the club and the bayonet are at hand ready to drive you to prison or the rope if you go beyond the established lines. Who can feel it more than a representative of the states? For the state owes its respect abroad to its fighting power more than to anything else. The world grew more careful of the United States after the achievement of our guest. As the public force gets more organized and complete the need of actually calling it forth grows correspondingly less. But the silence of unquestioned power and the dumbness of anarchy are as far apart as the infinite and zero.

SOURCE: a manuscript copy, in Holmes's hand, preserved among the Holmes papers at the Harvard Law School. A notation indicates that the prepared remarks were not in fact delivered.

The possibility of having to face death in battle which throughout all history has been in the background of mens' outlook upon life has given shape and color to what at this day we most value in men. The men of England are nerved and braced to a high heroic way of taking life by the little fights that she always is carrying somewhere upon her borders. They are quite as keen as other people for money and their personal advantage. But they will lay down their life without questions and in silence to uphold the Empire.

When I hear people talk about civil life as needing and teaching a courage equal to that of war, I feel very sure that I am listening to a noncombatant who never has known what it is to expect a bullet in his bowels in thirty seconds or to sail an iron clad over a mine.

People dwell on the sorrows of war. I know what they are. I saw my share of them when I was young with the Army of the Potomac. I shudder at them. I abhor the jingo spirit. I would do all that might be done honorably to avoid them. But the horrors of war after all are bodily suffering, the loss of property, and the loss of life. There are spiritual losses that are a thousand times worse. It is worse to be a coward than to lose an arm. It is better to be killed than to have a flabby soul. The true teaching of life is a tender hardheartedness which has passed beyond sympathy and which expects every man to abide his lot as he is able to shape it.

I look on these celebrations of our Admiral as a war song coming from the very heart of the people singing of a hero and great deeds with the faith out of which such deeds come and worshipping anew the symbol of tradition and prophecy—of union and power—of life, yes and of death not basely shunned—the flag under which we live and for which Dewey was ready to die.

WALBRIDGE ABNER FIELD

Answer to Resolutions of the Bar,
Boston, November 25, 1899

GENTLEMEN OF THE BAR: It is not easy to speak for the bench upon an event like that for which we meet. We judges are brought together so closely, I sat by the side of the late Chief Justice so long—it was nearly seventeen years—that separation has in it something too intimate for speech. Long association makes friendship, as it makes property and belief, a part of our being. When it is wrenched from us, roots are torn and broken that bleed like veins. Nevertheless we must not be silent when we are called to honor the memory of a remarkable man, although he was a brother. We must sink the private in the public loss.

Chief Justice Field was remarkable and was remarked from a very early age. His extraordinary reputation in his college was a prophecy of his later career. It may happen that a man is first scholar in his class, or whatever may be the modern equivalent of that now vanished distinction, solely by memory, powers of acquisition, and a certain docility of mind that too readily submits to direction and leadership. It may be, although I doubt it, that the chances are that some one in the field will outrun the favorite in the long race. It sometimes occurs that young men discount their future and exhaust their life in what, after all, is only preparation and not an end. But the presence of one great faculty does not argue the absence of others. The chances are that a man who leads in college will be a leader in after life. The chances are that the powers which carry a man to the front upon the prepared track will be accompanied by what is needed to give him at least an honorable place in the great gallop across the world. The usual happened with Chief Justice Field. He was always an important man, at the bar as well as later on the bench. It is a pleasure to me to remember that the first case which I ever had of my own was tried in the Superior Court before Judge Lord, whom afterwards I succeeded on this bench, and was argued before this court on the other side by Mr. Field. It is a pleasure to remember kind words and pleasant relations at that time. But of course those recollections are more or less swamped in those of a long intercourse here.

His mind was a very peculiar one. In the earlier days of my listening to him in consultation he seemed to me to think aloud, perhaps too much so, and to be unable to pass without mention the side suggestions which pressed in upon him in exuberant abundance. This very abundance made his work much harder to him. It was hard for him to neglect the possibilities of a side alley, however likely it might be to turn out a *cul-de-sac*. He wanted to know where it led before he passed it by. If we had eternity ahead this would be right and even necessary. But as life has but a short number of working hours, we have to choose at our peril; we have to act on the presumptions afforded by our present knowledge as to what paths are most likely to lead to desired goals. If we investigate Mohammedanism, or Spiritualism, or whether Bacon wrote Shakespeare, we have so much less time for philosophy, or church, or literature at large. So in deciding a question of law, one has to consider this element of time. One has to try to strike the jugular and let the rest go. I think that the Chief Justice did a vast deal of work which never appeared, in thus satisfying his conscience and in his unwillingness to risk leaving something out. You see the same characteristic in the statements of fact in his judgments. There is an elaborateness of detail about them which illustrates the tendency of his mind. If this exuberance was a fault, it was diminished as time went on. Without abating his care he gradually learned to omit.

Outside the law his fertility of mind made him a most interesting and delightful companion. He talked little about people, and never maliciously, but in the field of general ideas he roamed with freedom. He was discursive, humorous, skeptical by temperament, yet having convictions which gave steadiness to his thought. He had an extraordinary gift of repartee, and I used to delight in giving him opportunities to exercise it at my expense, for his answers were sure to be amusing and they never stung. No man ever had less bitterness in his nature. No man ever had a sweeter temper. I do not know how much it may have cost him to attain it, but it really was enough to bring tears to one's eyes to see how imperturbable he was in his amiability, no matter what grounds he might have for just irritation, no matter how much he might be suffering from fatigue and pain. His alleviating humor and his wit shone not merely in the consultation room, but elsewhere. I never have heard better after-dinner speeches than those which he would turn off with little or no preparation.

I have said that, although of skeptical temperament, he had convictions. The fact led to a curious result in his way of regarding the authority of decided cases. I am not sure how he would have expressed it, or indeed whether the notion was articulate in his mind, but he seemed to me to conceive of the law as ideally, at least, embodying absolute right. If a case appeared to him to run against some general principle which he thought was or ought to be a part of the law, the fact that it was decided seemed to make but little impression on his mind. He did not hesitate to throw doubt upon it or to disregard it. I do not think that he would have been content to regard the law as an empirical product of history, the particular forms of which are venerable mainly because they are—because in fact these and not something else which would seem to be as good or better if only the world were accustomed to it, are what our part of the world has come out on. Perhaps it was the same point of view that made him more ready than some judges to hold rather a tight rein upon the actual practices of the community. If a contract struck him as aiming at a gambling result, he would not enforce it, however much his refusal might encounter the daily practice of a whole board of brokers. He had his views of policy, and he did not doubt that the law agreed with him.

It was part of the same general habit of mind that he should be free to the point of innovation in applying convenient analogies to new cases. He sometimes seemed to me to go not only beyond but against tradition in his wish to render more perfect justice. He was less interested in the embryology of the law as an object of abstract speculation, or in the logical outcome of precedent, than he was in making sure that every interest should be represented before the court, and in extending useful remedies—a good fault, if it be a fault at all. He had an accomplished knowledge of the present state of the law, and a good deal of curious and useful information about our local history, for which I have envied him often. I doubt if any lawyer whom I have known, except his honored predecessor, from whom we still learn upon another bench, was his equal in this regard.

The personal characteristics which I have mentioned went no further than to mark a person. They were no more than what every strong man has and must have. They were governed by excellent sense, moderation, and insight. He sometimes was so possessed by an idea, or special aspect of a case, as to be for a time inaccessible to suggestion until the fire had burned itself out; but in a little while, in two or three days if not the same day, he fully grasped and did justice to the other view. As a rule he was very quick and took an idea in a flash.

Men carry their signatures upon their persons, although they may not always be visible at the first glance. If you had looked casually at the Chief Justice you might not have seen more than a strong man like others. But to a more attentive watch there came out a high intellectual radiance that was all his own. I have caught myself over and over again staring with delight upon his profile as I sat beside him, and admiring the fine keenness of his thought-absorbed gaze.

He had the heroic temper. This is the last, the greatest, thing that I can say. I used to notice, even in little matters, that he always looked his own conduct in the face and did not equivocate, apologize, or disguise. I could not notice, because it was too hidden, but I know, that he did his work in the same great way. It is hard to realize or believe what sufferings he went through long before the end. But if he had walked the floor all night in poignant pain, when he appeared in the morning he gave no sign of it unless it may be by silence. He took his work hard, as I have intimated, but he never said so, and he went down fighting, like a brave man as he was.

Gentlemen, for all of us this is a solemn moment. For me it is almost oppressively solemn. It would be serious enough were I only to remember the line of great, gifted, and good men whose place I have been called on to fill. But it is sadly, yes, awfully solemn, when I remember that with our beloved chief vanishes the last of those who were upon the bench when I took my seat, and so realize the swift, monotonous iteration of death. We sometimes wonder at the interest of mankind in platitudes. It is because truths realized are truths rediscovered, and each of us with advancing years realizes in his own experience what he always has admitted but never before has felt. The careless boy admits that life is short, but he feels that a term in college, a summer vacation, a day, is long. We gray-haired men hear in our ears the roar of the cataract and know that we are very near. The cry of personal anguish is almost drowned by the resounding echo of universal fate. It has become easier for us to imagine even the time when the cataract will be still, the race of men will be no more, and the great silence shall be supreme. What then may be the value of our judgments of significance and worth I know not. But I do firmly believe that if those judgments are not, as they may be, themselves the *flammantia moenia mundi*, the bounds and governance of all being, it is only because they are swallowed up and dissolved in something unimaginable and greater out of which they emerged. Our last word about the unfathomable universe must be in terms of thought. If we believe that anything is, we must believe in that, because we can go no further. We may accept its canons even while we admit that we do not know that we know the truth of truth. Accepting them, we accept our destiny to work, to fight, to die for ideal aims. At the grave of a hero who has done these things we end not with sorrow at the inevitable loss, but with the contagion of his courage; and with a kind of desperate joy we go back to the fight.

DR. S. WEIR MITCHELL

Remarks at a Tavern Club Dinner,
March 4, 1900

MR. CHAIRMAN: It is for others to give their appreciation, so far as may be consistent with the modesty of our guest, of his double achievement in science and in literature. We have here distinguished doctors and the writers of successful books. It is for them to speak according to their calling of what our guest has done in each. For I doubt if any one man would assume for himself even a corner of Dr. Mitchell's mantle large enough to cover him in the attempt to do justice to both. I offer my few words of welcome in the more modest capacity of the representative of another doctor, who in his day, I am encouraged to believe, paid his debt to his profession, and who also was not unknown in letters. It was a pleasure and pride of his later years to call Dr. Mitchell his friend. His son would be wanting in human feeling if he did not join in this occasion with a full heart.

I shall venture for a moment away from the field of personal reflections. It seems to me that in one sense the

SOURCE: a manuscript, in Holmes's hand, preserved among the Holmes papers at the Harvard Law School.

Silas Weir Mitchell (1829–1914), Philadelphia physician, neurologist, and novelist, was a long-time friend of Dr. Holmes's.

sphere of literature is narrowing. Art and religion, in spite of their kinship, long have lived under separate roofs. Law left the hands of the priests even further back. Today the whole domain of truth concerning the visible world belongs to science. One half resents sporadic *aperçus* about the universe because he discerns that they are fragments of an actual or possible science. It no longer would be possible for any but superficial persons to repeat Mrs. Browning's attitudinizing exclamation concerning the poets: "I speak of the only truth-tellers now left to God." We know that God is not so hard up as she professed to think. We yield but scant sympathy to Tennyson's posing

> Vex not thou the poet's mind
> With thy shallow wit

We know that the epoch-making ideas have come not from the poets but from the philosophers, the jurists, the mathematicians, the physicists, the doctors—from the men who explain, not from the men who feel. We realize that explanation and feeling are at the opposite poles of intellectual life, and require and come from opposite interests and opposite gifts. We no longer ask of *belles lettres* that they should be a "criticism of life," in Matthew Arnold's phrase, or that they should help us to fix our attitude toward the world. We do not read novels for improvement or instruction. We do not want "medicated fiction"—to quote what once was said to my father—we want only to be amused, to be moved, to be uplifted, and to be charmed.

To my mind the great realistic movement is perfectly

consistent with what I have said. The end of art is to pull the trigger of an emotion. But what will pull the trigger depends upon the audience. If they know too much to believe a ghost story even for half an hour, there is no use in telling them ghost stories. If the instantaneous photograph has made them notice more exactly how animals move, the old pictures of races, in which the horses' legs stuck out straight fore and aft, no longer give them this feeling of speed, and the pictures miss their end. Realism seeks more truth, not because truth is the end of art, but because at the present day more truth is the condition of our feeling what the artist wants to make us feel.

So I say that there has been a further differentiation of callings; that art no longer is a handyman about the house, with a general business of imparting useful information, but that it more and more definitely is and will be confined to the function of making us feel what it is for others to prove and in the main to discover. For the most part thinkers belong in the opposite camp. Few indeed are the men who unite in any degree the power to disclose truth and the power to make it live in our hearts. Few are they who at once can reveal and charm.

I have made these general reflections, partly because they naturally came into my mind when I think of literature, and because, while no general proposition is worth a straw, the chief end of man is to frame them, but mainly in honor of our guest, who presents so very unusual an example of success at both the poles. A man must indeed command large forces who can turn both flanks of the enemy and not himself be cut in two.

SPEECH

At a Dinner Given to Chief Justice Holmes
By the Bar Association of Boston
On March 7, 1900

GENTLEMEN OF THE SUFFOLK BAR: The kindness of this reception almost unmans me, and it shakes me the more when taken with a kind of seriousness which the moment has for me. As with a drowning man, the past is telescoped into a minute, and the stages are all here at once in my mind. The day before yesterday I was at the law school, fresh from the army, arguing cases in a little club with Goulding and Beaman and Peter Olney, and laying the dust of pleading by certain sprinklings which Huntington Jackson, another ex-soldier, and I managed to contrive together. A little later in the day, in Bob Morse's office, I saw a real writ, acquired a practical conviction of the difference between assumpsit and trover, and marvelled open-mouthed at the swift certainty with which a master of his business turned it off.

Yesterday I was at the law school again, in the chair instead of on the benches, when my dear partner, Shattuck, came out and told me that in one hour the Governor would submit my name to the council for a judgeship, if notified of my assent. It was a stroke of lightning which changed the whole course of my life.

And the day before yesterday, gentlemen, was thirty-five years, and yesterday was more than eighteen years, ago. I have gone on feeling young, but I have noticed that I met fewer of the old to whom to show my deference, and recently I was startled by being told that ours is an old bench. Well, I accept the fact, although I find it hard to realize, and I ask myself, what is there to show for this half lifetime that has passed? I look into my book in which I keep a docket of the decisions of the full court which fall to me to write, and find about a thousand cases. A thousand cases, many of them upon trifling or transitory matters, to represent nearly half a lifetime! A thousand cases, when one would have liked to study to the bottom and to say his say on every question which the law ever has presented, and then to go on and invent new problems which should be the test of doctrine, and then to generalize it all and write it in continuous, logical, philosophic exposition, setting forth the whole corpus with its roots in history and its justifications of expedience real or supposed!

Alas, gentlemen, that is life. I often imagine Shakespeare or Napoleon summing himself up and thinking: "Yes, I have written five thousand lines of solid gold and a good deal of padding—I, who would have covered the milky way with words which outshone the stars!" "Yes, I beat the Austrians in Italy and elsewhere: I made a few brilliant campaigns, and I ended in middle life in a *cul-de-sac*—I, who had dreamed of a world monarchy and Asiatic power." We cannot live our dreams. We are lucky enough if we can give a sample of our best, and if in our hearts we can feel that it has been nobly done.

Some changes come about in the process, changes not necessarily so much in the nature as in the emphasis of our interest. I do not mean in our wish to make a living and to succeed—of course, we all want those things—but I mean in our ulterior intellectual or spiritual interest, in the ideal part, without which we are but snails or tigers.

One begins with a search for a general point of view. After a time he finds one, and then for a while he is absorbed in testing it, in trying to satisfy himself whether it is true. But after many experiments or investigations all have come out one way, and his theory is confirmed and settled in his mind, he knows in advance that the next case will be but another verification, and the stimulus of anxious curiosity is gone. He realizes that his branch of knowledge only presents more illustrations of the universal principle; he sees it all as another case of the same old ennui, or the same sublime mystery—for it does not matter what epithets you apply to the whole of things, they are merely judgments of yourself. At this stage the pleasure is no less, perhaps, but it is the pure pleasure of doing the work, irrespective of further aims, and when you reach that stage you reach, as it seems to me, the triune formula of the joy, the duty, and the end of life.

It was of this that Malebranche was thinking when he said that, if God held in one hand truth, and in the other the pursuit of truth, he would say: "Lord, the truth is for thee alone; give me the pursuit." The joy of life is to put out one's power in some natural and useful or harmless way. There is no other. And the real misery is not to do this. The hell of the old world's literature is to be taxed beyond one's powers. This country has expressed in story—I suppose because it has experienced it in life—a deeper abyss, of intellectual asphyxia or vital ennui, when powers conscious of themselves are denied their chance.

The rule of joy and the law of duty seem to me all one. I confess that altruistic and cynically selfish talk seem to me about equally unreal. With all humility, I think "Whatsoever thy hand findeth to do, do it with thy might," infinitely more important than the vain attempt to love one's neighbor as one's self. If you want to hit a bird on the wing, you must have all your will in a focus, you must not be thinking about yourself, and, equally, you must not be thinking about your neighbor; you must be living in your eye on that bird. Every achievement is a bird on the wing.

The joy, the duty, and, I venture to add, the end of life. I speak only of this world, of course, and of the teachings of this world. I do not seek to trench upon the province of spiritual guides. But from the point of view of the world the end of life is life. Life is action, the use of one's powers. As to use them to their height is our joy and duty, so it is the one end that justifies itself. Until lately the best thing that I was able to think of in favor of civilization, apart from blind acceptance of the order of the universe, was that it made possible the artist, the poet, the philosopher, and the man of science.

But I think that is not the greatest thing. Now I believe that the greatest thing is a matter that comes directly home to us all. When it is said that we are too much occupied with the means of living to live, I answer that the chief worth of civilization is just that it makes the means of living more complex; that it calls for great and combined intellectual efforts, instead of simple, uncoördinated ones, in order that the crowd may be fed and clothed and housed and moved from place to place. Because more complex and intense intellectual efforts mean a fuller and richer life. They mean more life. Life is an end in itself, and the only question as to whether it is worth living is whether you have enough of it.

I will add but a word. We all are very near despair. The sheathing that floats us over its waves is compounded of hope, faith in the unexplainable worth and sure issue of effort, and the deep, sub-conscious content which comes from the exercise of our powers. In the words of a touching negro song—

> Sometimes I's up, sometimes I's down,
> Sometimes I's almost to the groun';

but these thoughts have carried me, as I hope they will carry the young men who hear me, through long years of doubt, self-distrust, and solitude. They do now, for, although it might seem that the day of trial was over, in fact it is renewed each day. The kindness which you have shown me makes me bold in happy moments to believe that the long and passionate struggle has not been quite in vain.

WILLIAM CROWNINSHIELD ENDICOTT

Answer to Resolutions of the Bar,
Boston, November 24, 1900

GENTLEMEN OF THE BAR: It is November and the last leaves are falling that once screened my generation from the sky. When I began my practice Mr. Endicott was the leader of the Essex bar. He left the bench a little before I came to it and in the same year. I caught some glimpses of him in both capacities, as a lawyer and as a judge. When I was still very young, for some reason which I never could explain except by his kindness, he called me into a case which he was going to try in Boston, as his junior. It was a case involving, if I remember rightly, some of those dealings of builders and contractors which are enough to puzzle or at least confuse older heads than mine was then. I fear that I never understood it and that I was but little help to him. But it taught me more than one lesson. The thoroughness of his preparation, the calmness with which he separated and drew out the tangled threads, the luminous ardor

SOURCE: 177 Mass. 612.

William Crowninshield Endicott was Associate Justice of the Supreme Judicial Court of Massachusetts, from 1873 to 1882, and Secretary of War in Cleveland's cabinet, 1885–1888.

with which he put his case to the jury, all were enough to inspire a neophyte with enthusiasm. And then his consideration for me, his manners to all—a wonderful contrast to much that then was tolerated. I am happy to think that his example has prevailed and that now it is the rule that a lawyer will try his case like a gentleman without giving up any portion of his energy and force.

When next I saw him it was upon the bench, and again he excited my admiration. He was sitting in the old equity courtroom in Court Square, and I remember thinking at the time, as I still think, that he represented in the superlative degree my notion of the proper bearing and conduct of a judge. Distinguished in person, with the look of race in his countenance which in more ways than one suggested a resemblance to that first Endicott to whom Massachusetts owes so much, he sat without a thought of self, without even the unconscious pride or aloofness which seemed, nay, was, his right, serenely absorbed in the problems of the matter in hand, impersonal yet human, the living image of justice, weighing as if the elements in the balance were dead matter, but discerning and collecting those elements by the help of a noble and tender heart. Ah, me! How often I have wished that one of his successors could attain the perfection which once he saw in the flesh! How often has that charming and impressive figure risen before my eyes, at once to encourage and to warn.

He was not less successful in the performance of his other duties as a judge. He was thought to have great power over juries—a matter of more importance in this court then than now, as in his day more jury cases were tried here. Among other causes, the jurisdiction in actions of torts still was retained, and murders continued to be tried before two judges of this bench until long after I came to it. Even under our unfortunate legislation, in his mode of presenting the different hypotheses and stating the law according to what the jury may find, a judge inevitably adopts such an order and such an emphasis as to bring to their attention what he deems the important elements of the case, and by so doing inevitably in some degree helps to lead them to what he thinks the proper result. I never heard Judge Endicott complained of as going too far, but I think it was recognized that the jury was likely to come out in the way that he thought right.

As a writer of decisions of the full court, I cannot estimate him as accurately as I could wish, because my other duties have not allowed me time to study his work with a view to critical appreciation. When one reads cases in the way of business, one is intent upon other things than the personality of the man who happens to express the judgment of the court. I think of him as not avoiding the difficulties of a case, as not seeking refuge in generalities, as clear in exposition, and as agreeable to read. Beyond that I should not undertake to speak. I have been led to surmise that he found the labor of writing too great, and that this was the reason for his resignation. That is a matter of temperament. The work here has killed some men who took it too hard. But I should not have supposed that Judge Endicott found it other than easy, from his style.

I shall not speak of his important political place after

he left this court, for the reason that I know too little about it, but shall content myself with saying that as I saw and knew him upon the bench, of the many interesting, powerful, and impressive figures that now are only memories, his stands out unique in dignity and charm.

JOHN MARSHALL

In Answer to a Motion that the Court Adjourn, On February 4, 1901, the One Hundredth Anniversary of the Day on Which Marshall Took His Seat as Chief Justice

As WE walk down Court Street in the midst of a jostling crowd, intent like us upon to-day and its affairs, our eyes are like to fall upon the small, dark building that stands at the head of State Street, and, like an ominous reef, divides the stream of business in its course to the gray cliffs that tower beyond. And, whoever we may be, we may chance to pause and forget our hurry for a moment, as we remember that the first waves that foretold the coming storm of the Revolution broke around that reef. But, if we are lawyers, our memories and our reverence grow more profound. In the old State House, we remember, James Otis argued the case of the writs of assistance, and in that argument laid one of the foundations for American constitutional law. Just as that little building is not diminished, but rather is enhanced and glorified, by the vast structures which somehow it turns into a background, so the beginnings of our national life, whether in battle or in law, lose none of their greatness by contrast with all the mighty things of later date, beside which, by every law of number and measure, they ought to seem so small. To us who took part in the Civil

War, the greatest battle of the Revolution seems little more than a reconnoissance in force, and Lexington and Concord were mere skirmishes that would not find mention in the newspapers. Yet veterans who have known battle on a modern scale, are not less aware of the spiritual significance of those little fights, I venture to say, than the enlightened children of commerce who tell us that soon war is to be no more.

If I were to think of John Marshall simply by number and measure in the abstract, I might hesitate in my superlatives, just as I should hesitate over the battle of the Brandywine if I thought of it apart from its place in the line of historic cause. But such thinking is empty in the same proportion that it is abstract. It is most idle to take a man apart from the circumstances which, in fact, were his. To be sure, it is easier in fancy to separate a person from his riches than from his character. But it is just as futile. Remove a square inch of mucous membrane, and the tenor will sing no more. Remove a little cube from the brain, and the orator will be speechless; or another, and the brave, generous, and profound spirit becomes a timid and querulous trifler. A great man represents a great ganglion in the nerves of society, or, to vary the figure, a strategic point in the campaign of history, and part of his greatness consists in his being *there*. I no more can separate John Marshall from the fortunate circumstance that the appointment of Chief Justice fell to John Adams, instead of to Jefferson a month later, and so gave it to a Federalist and loose constructionist to start the working of the Constitution, than I can separate the black line through which he sent his electric fire at Fort Wagner from Colonel Shaw. When we celebrate Marshall we celebrate at the same time and indivisibly the inevitable fact that the oneness of the nation and the supremacy of the national Constitution were declared to govern the dealings of man with man by the judgments and decrees of the most august of courts.

I do not mean, of course, that personal estimates are useless or teach us nothing. No doubt to-day there will be heard from able and competent persons such estimates of Marshall. But I will not trench upon their field of work. It would be out of place when I am called on only to express the answer to a motion addressed to the court and when many of those who are here are to listen this afternoon to the accomplished teacher who has had every occasion to make a personal study of the judge, and again this evening to a gentleman who shares by birth the traditions of the man. My own impressions are only those that I have gathered in the common course of legal education and practice. In them I am conscious, perhaps, of some little revolt from our purely local or national estimates, and of a wish to see things and people judged by more cosmopolitan standards. A man is bound to be parochial in his practice—to give his life, and if necessary his death, for the place where he has his roots. But his thinking should be cosmopolitan and detached. He should be able to criticize what he reveres and loves.

The *Federalist*, when I read it many years ago, seemed to me a truly original and wonderful production for the time. I do not trust even that judgment unrevised when

I remember that the *Federalist* and its authors struck a distinguished English friend of mine as finite; and I should feel a greater doubt whether, after Hamilton and the Constitution itself, Marshall's work proved more than a strong intellect, a good style, personal ascendancy in his court, courage, justice, and the convictions of his party. My keenest interest is excited, not by what are called great questions and great cases, but by little decisions which the common run of selectors would pass by because they did not deal with the Constitution or a telephone company, yet which have in them the germ of some wider theory, and therefore of some profound interstitial change in the very tissue of the law. The men whom I should be tempted to commemorate would be the originators of transforming thought. They often are half obscure, because what the world pays for is judgment, not the original mind.

But what I have said does not mean that I shall join in this celebration or in granting the motion before the court in any half-hearted way. Not only do I recur to what I said in the beginning, and remembering that you cannot separate a man from his place, remember also that there fell to Marshall perhaps the greatest place that ever was filled by a judge; but when I consider his might, his justice, and his wisdom, I do fully believe that if American law were to be represented by a single figure, skeptic and worshipper alike would agree without dispute that the figure could be but one alone, and that one John Marshall.

A few words more and I have done. We live by symbols, and what shall be symbolized by any image of the sight depends upon the mind of him who sees it. The setting aside of this day in honor of a great judge may stand to a Virginian for the glory of his glorious State; to a patriot for the fact that time has been on Marshall's side, and that the theory for which Hamilton argued, and he decided, and Webster spoke, and Grant fought, and Lincoln died, is now our corner-stone. To the more abstract but farther-reaching contemplation of the lawyer, it stands for the rise of a new body of jurisprudence, by which guiding principles are raised above the reach of statute and State, and judges are entrusted with a solemn and hitherto unheard-of authority and duty. To one who lives in what may seem to him a solitude of thought, this day—as it marks the triumph of a man whom some Presidents of his time bade carry out his judgments as he could—this day marks the fact that all thought is social, is on its way to action; that, to borrow the expression of a French writer, every idea tends to become first a catechism and then a code; and that according to its worth his unhelped meditation may one day mount a throne, and without armies, or even with them, may shoot across the world the electric despotism of an unresisted power. It is all a symbol, if you like, but so is the flag. The flag is but a bit of bunting to one who insists on prose. Yet, thanks to Marshall and to the men of his generation—and for this above all we celebrate him and them—its red is our life-blood, its stars our world, its blue our heaven. It owns our land. At will it throws away our lives.

The motion of the bar is granted, and the court will now adjourn.

IPSWICH

At the Unveiling of Memorial Tablets,
July 31, 1902

We are told by scholars that the Greeks and Romans built up their cities and their civilization on the worship of their ancestors and care for the shadowy needs of the dead. That ancient religion has vanished, but the reverence for venerable traditions remains. I feel it to my finger tips, but with just the change from personal and family story to the larger, vaguer, but not less inspiring belief that we tread a sacred soil. I have been too busy trying to account for myself to stop to account for my ancestors. I have the poems of Ann Bradstreet, that pale passion flower of our first spring, but I do not read them often, and I cannot say much more of Governor Dudley than that what I once wrongly thought his portrait, in modest form, hangs in my house. But I love every brick and shingle of the old Massachusetts towns where once they worked and prayed, and I think it a noble and pious thing to do whatever we may by written word and molded bronze and sculptured stone to keep our memories, our reverence, and our love alive and to hand them on to new generations all too ready to forget.

It may be that we are to be replaced by other races

that come here with other traditions and to whom at first the great past of Massachusetts seems, as they sometimes proclaim it, but the doings in a corner of a little band of provincial heretics. But I am bold to hope that the mighty leaven that swelled the hearts of the founders of this Commonwealth still works and will work even under altered forms—that their successors will keep the state what the founders made it, a hearthstone for sacred fire.

We all, the most unbelieving of us, walk by faith. We do our work and live our lives not merely to vent and realize our inner force, but with a blind and trembling hope that somehow the world will be a little better for our striving. Our faith must not be limited to our personal task; to the present, or even to the future. It must include the past and bring all, past, present, and future, into the unity of a single continuous life. We consecrate these memorials of what has been with the intent and expectation that centuries from now those who read the simple words will find their lives richer, their purposes stronger, against the background of that different past.

From early days there have been built in the ports of Essex County, or drawn to them from neighboring towns, boats that were to seek from them new harbors across the barren sea. So, in altered guise, long may it be with us. Long may it be true, as it still is, that not only we, descendants of the stern old builders, but many others from afar who come here to launch their craft, may send to all the havens of the world new thoughts and the impulses of great deeds. To the accomplishment of that prayer it is no slight help to feel that we have a past, to remember that many generations of men have stored the earth—yes, this very spot—with electric example. Modest as they are, the monuments now unveiled seem to me trumpets which two hundred years from now may blow the great battle calls of life, as two hundred years ago those whom they commemorate heard them in their hearts. And to many a gallant spirit, two hundred years from now as two hundred years ago, the white sands of Ipswich, terrible as engulfing graves, lovely as the opal flash of fairy walls, will gleam in the horizon, the image of man's mysterious goal.

ADDRESS

At the Dedication of the
Northwestern University Law School Building,
Chicago, October 20, 1902

MR. PRESIDENT AND GENTLEMEN: Nature has but one judgment on wrong conduct—if you can call that a judgment which seemingly has no reference to conduct as such—the judgment of death. That is the judgment or the consequence which follows uneconomical expenditure if carried far enough. If you waste too much food you starve; too much fuel, you freeze; too much nerve tissue, you collapse. And so it might seem that the law of life is the law of the herd; that man should produce food and raiment in order that he might produce yet other food and other raiment to the end of time. Yet who does not rebel at that conclusion? Accepting the premises, I nevertheless almost am prepared to say that every joy that gives to life its inspiration consists in an excursion toward death, although wisely stopping short of its goal. Art, philosophy, charity, the search for the

SOURCE: *Collected Legal Papers* (New York, 1920), p. 272. The address is reprinted here with the permission of the copyright owner, Harcourt, Brace & Company.

The dean of the Northwestern Law School was Professor John H Wigmore.

north pole, the delirium of every great moment in man's experience—all alike mean uneconomic expenditure—mean waste—mean a step toward death. The justification of art is not that it offers prizes to those who succeed in the economic struggle, to those who in an economic sense have produced the most, and that thus by indirection it increases the supply of wine and oil. The justification is in art itself, whatever its economic effect. It gratifies an appetite which in some noble spirits is stronger than the appetite for food. The principle might be pressed even further and be found to furnish art with one of its laws. For it might be said, as I often have said, and as I have been gratified to find elaborated by that true poet Coventry Patmore, that one of the grounds of aesthetic pleasure is waste. I need not refer to Charles Lamb's well-known comments on the fallacy that enough is as good as a feast. Who does not know how his delight has been increased to find some treasure of carving upon a mediaeval cathedral in a back alley—to see that the artist has been generous as well as great, and has not confined his best to the places where it could be seen to most advantage? Who does not recognize the superior charm of a square-hewed beam over a joist set on edge which would be enough for the work? To leave art, who does not feel that Nansen's account of his search for the pole rather loses than gains in ideal satisfaction by the pretense of a few trifling acquisitions for science? If I wished to make you smile I might even ask whether life did not gain an enrichment from neglected opportunities which would be missed in the snug filling out of every chance. But I am not here to press a paradox. I only mean to insist on the importance of the uneconomic to man as he actually feels to-day. You may philosophize about the honors of leisure as a survival; you may, if you like, describe in the same way, as I have heard them described, the ideals which burn in the center of our hearts. None the less they are there. They are categorical imperatives. They hold their own against hunger and thirst; they scorn to be classed as mere indirect supports of our bodily needs, which rather they defy; and our friends the economists would do well to take account of them, as some great writers like M. Tarde would take account of them, if they are to deal with man as he is. No doubt already you have perceived the reason why I have insisted upon this double view of life. The special value of a university is that it moves in the twofold direction of man's desires which I have described. I have listened with interest to able business men when they argued and testified that a university training made men fitter to succeed in their practical struggles. I am far from denying it. No doubt such a training gives men a larger mastery of the laws of nature under which they must work, a wider outlook over the world of science and of fact. If it could give to every student a scientific point of view, if education could make men realize that you cannot produce something out of nothing and make them promptly detect the pretense of doing so with which at present the talk of every day is filled, I should think it had more than paid for itself. Still more should I think so if it could send men into the world with a good rudimentary knowledge of the laws of their environment. I cannot believe that anything else would be so likely to secure prosperity as the universal acceptance of scientific premises in every department of thought. But beside prosperity there is to be considered happiness, which is not the same thing. The chance of a university to enlarge men's power of happiness is at least not less than its chance to enlarge their capacity for gain. I own that with regard to this, as with regard to every other aspiration of man, the most important question seems to me to be, what are his inborn qualities?

Mr. Ruskin's first rule for learning to draw, you will remember, was, Be born with genius. It is the first rule for everything else. If a man is adequate in native force, he probably will be happy in the deepest sense, whatever his fate. But we must not undervalue effort, even if it is the lesser half. And the opening which a university is sure to offer to all the idealizing tendencies—which, I am not afraid to say, it ought to offer to the romantic side of life—makes it above all other institutions the conservator of the vestal fire. Our tastes are finalities, and it has been recognized since the days of Rome that there is not much use in disputing about them. If some professor should proclaim that what he wanted was a strictly economic world, I should see no more use in debating with him than I do in arguing with those who despise the ideals which we owe to war. But most men at present are on the university side. They want to be told stories and to go to the play. They want to understand and, if they can, to paint pictures, and to write poems, whether the food product is greater in the long run because of them or not. They want to press philosophy to the uttermost edge of the articulate, and to try forever after some spiritual ray outside the spectrum that will bring a message to them from behind phenomena. They love the gallant adventure which yields no visible return. I think it the glory of that university which I know best, that under whatever reserves of manner they may hide it, its graduates have the romantic passion in their hearts.

But, gentlemen, there is one department of your institution to which I must be permitted specially to refer —the department to which I am nearest by profession, and to which I owe the honor of being here. I mean, of course, the department of law. Let me say one word about that before I sit down. It was affirmed, I believe, by a man not without deserved honor in his generation— the late Chief Justice Cooley—that the law was and ought to be commonplace. No doubt the remark has its truth. It is better that the law should be commonplace than that it should be eccentric. No doubt, too, in any aspect it would seem commonplace to a mind that understood everything. But that is the weakness of all truth. If instead of the joy of eternal pursuit you imagine yourself to have mastered it as a complete whole, you would find yourself reduced to the alternative either of finding the remotest achievement of quaternions or ontology— the whole frame of the universe, in short—a bore, or of dilating with undying joy over the proposition that twice two is four. It seems to me that for men as they are, the law may keep its every-day character and yet be an object of understanding wonder and a field for the lightning of genius. One reason why it gives me pleasure to be here today and to express my good wishes for the future and my appreciation of the past of your law school, is that it is here and in places like it that such wonder is kindled and that from it may fly sparks that shall set free in some genius his explosive message.

I am not dealing in generalities. I mean more than good will to a law school, simply because it is a law school. Indeed, I almost fear that the intellectual ferment of the better schools may be too potent an attraction to young men and seduce into the profession many who would be better elsewhere. But I am thinking of this law school and no other. I never have had an opportunity to give public expression to my sense of the value of the work of your accomplished dean. I have come in for my share of criticism from him, as also I have had from him words which have given me new courage on a lonely road. But my appreciation of what I have seen from his hands is untouched by personal relations. It is solely because I think that it is the duty of those who know to recognize the unadvertised first rate, that I wish now to express my respect for his great learning and originality and for the volume and delicacy of his production, which seem to me to deserve more distinct and public notice than, so far as I am aware, they have received. I feel quite sure, from his printed work, that his teaching will satisfy the twofold desire of man; that it will be enlightened with intelligent economic views and give men what they want to know when they go out to fight, but that also it will send them forth with a pennon as well as with a sword, to keep before their eyes in the long battle the little flutter that means ideals, honor, yes, even romance, in all the dull details.

DESPONDENCY AND HOPE

Remarks at a Dinner
of the Chicago Bar Association,
October 21, 1902

MR. CHAIRMAN AND GENTLEMEN: Only twice before in my life have I had a glimpse of your wonderful city. Once in 1867, with Mr. Cabot Lodge, not then a senator of the United States, on our way to try to shoot prairie chickens. We had met a perfidious friend who hoped we had thick boots, on account of the rattlesnakes. So we rose early, before even Chicago was awake, in the hope of buying some, and jumped a yard on the prairie every time a cricket stirred in the grass. But we were temperate and saw no snakes. The other time was in the course of a journey across the continent, when our beloved friend Huntington Jackson showed me the courts and introduced me to Mr. Fuller, then just nominated by the President for Chief Justice of the United States. Now, after hope deferred and under altered circumstances, I am here again. Under altered circumstances—for if the senate should be of the same mind as the President, this meeting marks for me the turn to the home stretch of the race. Some sad thoughts will come

SOURCE: 35 Chicago Legal News 82 (1902).

up at the moment. One feels as if the second stage of one's life—one's twenty years of work as a state judge—were up for judgment in its turn, and that there must be few who will take the trouble or find it worth the trouble to consider it with discrimination or to discover one's aims. Then, of course, most of us find it easy to despond. When a man is satisfied with himself it means that he has ceased to struggle and therefore has ceased to achieve. He is dead, and may be allowed the thin delight of reading his own obituary. But this occasion drowns out all the rats that gnaw at one within. In this place, in the midst of so much force and life and success, one would indeed be morbid if he did not hope, and were not ready to tell the younger men who hear him that the race is worth the running. A man is pretty sure to get his due share of appreciation, for, whether he speaks or is silent, the world generally finds him out. But while it is a delight to get praise that one deserves, the fiercest joy is in the doing. Those who run hardest probably have the least satisfaction with themselves, but they find, I am sure, that they know most of the joy of life when at top speed.

Some of you probably have read the story of Calumet K. There is a little love in it as an obligatory concession to what is expected in a novel, but the whole romance of the tale is in the getting an elevator built in time to break a corner in wheat. That is the universal romance of man—to face obstacles and to measure his force by the number that he overcomes. Force *in vacuo* is Hegel's pure being—it is pure nothing. I was struck by the distinction of a remark in a letter to me the other day, that the true path is the line of most resistance. Following a similar train of thought, I sometimes have amused myself with the imagination of a society for the preservation of abuses, with closed seasons and fixed times within which alone one was authorized to make the crooked straight. For nature always is self-defeating, and if you imagine a time when our ideal was achieved, and there was nothing left to be set right, what would become of man? The faculties which are his life, finding no place for their exercise, would dwindle and decay, and the joy of life, as we know it, would be at an end.

A judge in our day need not fear such an atrophy of his powers. He has his share of obstacles to overcome, and none the less if his decision is beyond appeal. If he aims at the highest, he must take risks. He must be superior to class prejudices and to his own prejudices. He must not stop at consecrated phrases, which in their day were a revelation, but which in time from their very felicity, tend to stop the endless necessary process of further analysis and advance. He must throw down his naked thought, unswaddled in pompous commonplaces, to take its chance for life. He must try to realize the paradox that it is not necessary to be heavy in order to have weight.

Gentlemen, I might go on, but you all know these things better than I can say them to you. Who dares flatter himself that he fills the requirements which I imagine for a great judge? All that I venture to say for myself is that I have done my best with delight for twenty years, that I think my standards are cosmopolitan, and that by those standards some of the aids to immediate success must be condemned. As I said at the beginning, it is very easy to despond. But the unexpected honor which you have done me, the more than cordiality and good will, the generous and delicate hospitality with which I have been received, made me dream for a moment that it is even easier to succeed, and that perhaps after all I have not failed. At all events, and to the end, succeed or fail, the fight is joy, and I shall long hear in it the trumpet of your cheer.

A PROVISIONAL ADIEU

Remarks at a Tavern Club Dinner,
November 14, 1902

GENTLEMEN: It is hard to bid a provisional adieu, conditioned on the action of the Senate. But feeling does not wait, and since August I have found myself feeling a great deal more than I should have supposed likely, had I speculated upon the matter in advance. The roots of sixty years strike deep, and they cannot be tugged at or cut off without pain. The mere burning of old papers which have cumbered and annoyed one for thirty years, while it gives one for a moment a sigh of freedom, makes one feel a little later that it is the freedom of a cut flower—one little root in the past is gone.

As my thoughts have been turned in this way toward the past, this meeting brings to my mind the contrast between the Boston that I remember and the Boston of today. At the one end is Bosworth Street. It used to be Montgomery Place—the place where I was born. The little steps at the bottom leading to Province Street are more venerable to me than the Cenotaph of Romulus. At the other end is the new Boston of Commonwealth Avenue and all the wilderness of palaces where once I

SOURCE: a manuscript copy, in Holmes's hand, preserved among the Holmes papers at the Harvard Law School.

fished with a pin hook. At this end is the Boston of this club. The Boston of my youth was the still half-Puritan Boston, with the "unutterable ennui" of its Sundays and the church bells which I still affectionately hate. And what makes the contrast come to my mind at this moment, it was a Boston with no statues, few pictures, little music outside the churches, and no Christmas. On Christmas the shops were open, business went on as usual, and many people gave their presents on New Year's Day. There were no statues, unless you count the little admiral taking the sun at the corner of State and what then was Broad Street, until Mr. Iasigi set up the two figurines that stand in Louisburg Square. I then learned what I never have doubted since that bad statues are better than no statues. They are points of interest, and give you something to think about. When the first real full-grown statue was set up, the statue of Franklin in front of the City Hall, the change began. I remember, by the way, that I then picked up my first intimations as to the tendency of my profession. An old Yankee who was trying to elbow his way through the crowd said, "Wal, you git on here pretty much the way a lawyer goes to hell—by degrees." The pictures, apart from the portraits, and the old masters which it would be a compliment to call fishy, to be seen in private houses, were the little collection at the top of the Athenaeum, of which the Allstons and perhaps a few Stuarts were about all that we now should remark.

The change from those barren surroundings to today is inseparably identified in my mind with the change from boyhood to age. In either aspect the beginning was a weary time, even though mitigated by Henry Bowditch's teachings in the rudiments of crime—ringing doorbells and playing devil's tricks at back doors—a weary time—a time of waiting for "some divine, far-off event."

The event came. There were more than one. I am thinking now more of spiritual than of external changes. College gave one an atmosphere. The war was a great moral experience. The first five or ten years of one's profession was another, and perhaps a greater one. One had not all the aids that there are now to realizing why the subject was worthy of the interest of an intelligent man. I think that I have done my share to make that plain. Yet within a few years a leader in one of the Southern bar associations seemed to think that an expression of mine—that the law was the greatest human document—needed explanation, if it was not a pure paradox. When I began it was not so easy as it is now to see that law, looked at through the stereoscope of history, is the story of our growth. It was not easy to put to oneself even the vaguer proposition that as the facts of the law are facts of the universe they are worthy of their share of the only intellectual interest there is—the interest of being seen in their universal relations. As I look back to those periods of misery, the war and the beginning of one's profession, I cannot forbear saying, as I always say when I have any beginners within hearing, that it is true that you grow—that you must go through that trial of wretched doubt—doubt as to your own significance, ignorance of even what question you want to ask—and that it is through faith and will—faith that there is a question and an answer—will to attain them—that one enters the door of life.

At last perhaps there comes, as it has come to so many of those who hear me, success. The doubts remain—but I will say no more of them. I think rather of the departure of the old ennui, and the wonderful change in all our surroundings. I think, too, of the happiness that has come with opportunity to put one's energy and to live hard. Most of all at this moment I think of the happiness that comes with friends—friends that I see here; friends that one has made in middle life, in place of a whole departed generation that fell in war or too early suffered the final defeat; friends of a later day, with whom one is young a second time; friends of this club, the club where all are friends. As I have hinted, this club marks to me the changes which I have seen, the difference between what I remember and the happy event. At the beginning, the Boston half stifled in its bonds—at the end a center where gaily meet philosophy, law, medicine, painting, music, and everything that can instruct or charm or uplift. Gaily meet—for here gaiety is not suspected to be a sin. I have not been able to come here often. It has been my misfortune, not my fault. But I have felt the horizon of life enriched by knowing that the club was here, and if I should be called on to depart, one of my sincerest regrets will be that I leave behind, no longer within my reach, the Tavern Club, the only Boston club to which I ever belonged.

TWENTY YEARS IN RETROSPECT

Speech at a Banquet of the Middlesex Bar Association, December 3, 1902

GENTLEMEN OF THE MIDDLESEX BAR: Goethe said that two wise men could tell each other all that they knew in a couple of days. I have been telling you what I think for twenty years, and it would be hopeless to try to surprise you now. I can only say a few words of provisional good-by.

This month sees the end of the twenty happiest years of my life, and the happiest of those happy years have been the last. I am associated on the bench with men, every one of whom is my personal friend, with men whose varied abilities, single-heartedness, and devotion to their task I admire, and we meet on terms of unrestrained mutual criticism in a common effort to develop the law in a worthy way—in a way worthy of the great traditions of the state. In the consultation room all is affectionate and free. It is not different with the other half of the law builders. I have before me a bar that has improved ever since I have known it. I confidently believe that your arguments surpass in brevity, point, and

SOURCE: a newspaper clipping preserved among the Holmes papers at the Harvard Law School.

style those which I used to hear from the leaders of an earlier day. And I do not stop there. I hope that I may add without self-delusion that the bar and the bench are not merely fellow workers—they are friends.

Well, gentlemen, it is a good deal of a wrench to leave old friends, to leave the memorials of the dead, to leave all the associations of a whole life for an unknown new world. I had one glimpse of the Supreme Court when I went on to argue a case before it, which is already ancient history. I remember thinking that it needed only a black boy with gold bangles, holding a leash of greyhounds at one end of the bench, to be a living picture by Paul Veronese. The capital, with its asphalt pavements, is not quite unknown to me. But my notion of Washington still is the notion of the Washington of war times, where mule teams sank to their knees in mud, where at every other door one saw signs bearing the words, "Embalming the Dead," with an occasional alleviation in the form of "Sample room in the rear."

At this moment, too, the work of twenty years comes up for judgment, and that also is not without its sadness. You are the judges, and even you are more likely to take your views from the accident of your professional needs than from a consideration of any general aspect of a man's work.

I have tried to see the law as an organic whole. I also have tried to see it as a reaction between tradition on the one side and the changing desires and needs of a community on the other. I have studied tradition in order that I might understand how it came to be what it is, and to estimate its worth with regard to our present needs; and my references to the Year Books often have had a skeptical end. I have considered the present tendencies and desires of society and have tried to realize that its different portions want different things, and that my business was to express not my personal wish, but the resultant, as nearly as I could guess, of the pressure of the past and the conflicting wills of the present. I have considered the social and economic postulates on which we frame the conception of our needs, and I have to see them in a dry light. It has seemed to me that certainty is an illusion, that we have few scientific data on which to affirm that one rule rather than another has the sanction of the universe, that we rarely could be sure that one tends more distinctly than its opposite to the survival and welfare of the society where it is practiced, and that the wisest are but blind guides.

But we have a great body of law which has at least this sanction that it exists. If one does not affirm that it is intrinsically better than a different body of principles which one could imagine, one can see an advantage which, if not the greatest, at least, is very great—that we know what it is. For this reason I am slow to assent to overruling a decision. Precisely my skepticism, my doubt as to the absolute worth of a large part of the system we administer, or of any other system, makes me very unwilling to increase the doubt as to what the court will do. I have noticed the opposite tendency in minds that regarded our corpus juris as an image, however faint, of the eternal law. Well, gentlemen, I will avoid the longwindedness which I have deplored in others, and will leave my case in your hands, not trying to state it, but knowing that when one's work is done, generally there is someone, sooner or later, who sees the aim and judges the success.

As I have said, I have felt very sad at the thought of all that I leave, and sad with the wonder whether the work of twenty years, on which I have spent the passion of my heart, will be adjudged to have been nobly done. I have felt sad, too, with a different sadness in thinking of the future. It is an adventure into the unknown. No man can go far who never sets down his foot until he knows that the sidewalk is under it. But, gentlemen, it is a great adventure, and that thought brings with it a mighty joy. To have the chance to do one's share in shaping the laws of the whole country spreads over one the hush that one used to feel when one was awaiting the beginning of a battle. One does not forget the danger, but if victory should come! Victory shall come—with that thought the personal apprehension grows dim. The forces of one's soul rally and gather to a point. One looks down the lines and catches the eye of friends—he waves his sword—it may be the last time for him or them—but the advance is about to begin. The troops are deployed. They will follow their leader. We will not falter, we will not fail. We will reach the earthworks if we live, and if we fall we will leave our spirit in those who follow, and they will not turn back. All is ready. Bugler, blow the charge.

REMARKS AT A MEETING OF THE SECOND ARMY CORPS ASSOCIATION

Washington, D.C., March 13, 1903

Comrades of the Second Army Corps: It seems to me that this meeting, in this place, must be more impressive and moving to me than it can be to almost any one of those who are here. I have been at work in other fields. To me the War has become a shadowy dream. And now, practically for the first time for nearly forty years, I see again the Potomac, I meet again for the first time the survivors of the great corps.

I leave to others to tell our memories. But there is something that I wish I could tell—a something more exalting, more ethereal, more word escaping than even our memories—a something which I see in the faces or find hidden in the hearts of those who have known battle and in which I would sum up what the war did for our souls. It is the romantic spirit. It is the fire of life. Those who have not known what it is to march straight to where you see the bullets striking may talk, if they like, about the trials of civil life being greater than those of war. They may be right. But the men who have been

Source: a manuscript copy, in Holmes's hand, preserved among the Holmes papers at the Harvard Law School.

soaked in a sea of death and who somehow have survived, have got something from it which has transfigured their world. They learned in a bitter school honor and faith. They knew the passion of life and the irony of fate.

My work is supposed to be dry. It certainly calls for the least impassioned judgments that a man can form. The very temperament of a judge is abstract. And yet even one of that temperament, one who has been through the long years of silent toil by which he was prepared for his task, and one who holds his opinions as coldly as mathematics, one who has forgotten all the pictures that once burned in upon his eyes—even such a one may yet remember and may say as he looks in your faces: It was with you that I learned the hardest and the noblest lessons of duty. It was by your side that I had kindled in my heart a fire that will not go out.

THE CLASS OF '61

At the Fiftieth Anniversary of Graduation, June 28, 1911

Mr. President and Brethren of the Alumni: One of the recurring sights of Alaska, I believe, is when a section of the great glacier cracks and drops into the sea. The last time that I remember witnessing the periodic semi-centennial plunge of a college class was when I heard Longfellow say "Morituri salutamus." If I should repeat that phrase of the gladiators soon to die, it would be from knowledge and reason, not from feeling, for I own that I am apt to wonder whether I do not dream that I have lived, and may not wake to find that all that I thought done is still to be accomplished and that life is all ahead. But we have had our warning. Even within the last three months Henry Bowditch, the world-known physiologist, and Frank Emmons, the world-known geologist, have dropped from the class, leaving only the shadow of great names.

I like to think that they were types of '61, not only in their deeds, but in their noble silence. It has been my fortune to belong to two bodies that seemed to me somewhat alike—the 20th Massachusetts Regiment and the class of '61. The 20th never wrote about itself to the newspapers, but for its killed and wounded in battle it stood in the first half-dozen of all the regiments of the north. This little class never talked much about itself, but graduating just as the war of secession began, out of its eighty-one members it had fifty-one under arms, the largest proportion that any class sent to that war.

One learns from time an amiable latitude with regard to beliefs and tastes. Life is painting a picture, not doing a sum. As twenty men of genius looking out of the same window will paint twenty canvases, each unlike all the others, and every one great, so, one comes to think, men may be pardoned for the defects of their qualities if they have the qualities of their defects. But, after all, we all of us have our notions of what is best. I learned in the regiment and in the class the conclusion, at least, of what I think the best service that we can do for our country and for ourselves: To see so far as one may, and to feel, the great forces that are behind every detail—for that makes all the difference between philosophy and gossip, between great action and small; the least wavelet of the Atlantic Ocean is mightier than one of Buzzard's Bay—to hammer out as compact and solid a piece of work as one can, to try to make it first rate, and to leave it unadvertised.

It was a good thing for us in our college days, as Moorfield Storey pointed out a few years ago in an excellent address, that we were all poor. At least we lived as if we were. It seems to me that the training at West Point is better fitted to make a man than for a youth to have all the luxuries of life poured into a trough for him at twenty. We had something of that discipline, and before it was over many of us were in barracks learning the school of the soldier. Man is born a predestined idealist, for he is born to act. To act is to affirm the worth of an end, and to persist in affirming the worth of an end is to make an ideal. The stern experience of our youth helped to accomplish the destiny of fate. It left us feeling through life that pleasures do not make happiness and that the root of joy as of duty is to put out all one's powers toward some great end.

When one listens from above to the roar of a great city, there comes to one's ears—almost indistinguishable, but there—the sound of church bells, chiming the hours, or offering a pause in the rush, a moment for withdrawal and prayer. Commerce has outsoared the steeples that once looked down upon the marts, but still their note makes music of the din. For those of us who are not churchmen the symbol still lives. Life is a roar of bargain and battle, but in the very heart of it there rises a mystic spiritual tone that gives meaning to the whole. It transmutes the dull details into romance. It reminds us that our only but wholly adequate significance is as parts of the unimaginable whole. It suggests that even while we think that we are egotists we are living to ends outside ourselves.

REFLECTIONS ON THE PAST AND FUTURE

Remarks at a Dinner of the Alpha Delta Phi Club, Cambridge, September 27, 1912

When I was a small boy and was allowed to see the celebrations of the day—it may have been on the introduction of the Cochituate water into Boston, or the funeral of John Quincy Adams, or I know not what—I was most impressed by the part played by a carload of veterans. I got the notion, which has persisted, that the glory of life was to be carried in a civic procession, in a barge, as a survivor—I did not inquire too curiously of what. Now I am beginning to realize that somber joy, and to feel something like the old gentleman of whom I overheard Judge Hoar tell, who remembered George Washington before dinner—and after dinner remembered Christopher Columbus. Take this Club. In my day, after having been saved from extinction by two members of the Class of 1860, it used to meet, I think rather oftener than elsewhere in my room, at Danforth's in Linden Street, which had the advantage of being outside the College Yard. If I am not mistaken, the last

Source: a manuscript copy, in Holmes's hand, preserved among the Holmes papers at the Harvard Law School.

meeting that I attended before this was there in 1860 or 1861. In those days the Club used to listen to essays by its members before the business of the bottle began. Without yet going back to Columbus it may connect you with the past if I mention that at that time my grandmother was alive and that she remembered moving out of Boston when the British troops came in, before the Revolution. I spoke of the introduction of Cochituate water. When I was a boy there were pumps in the back yards. The closets that depend upon the pipes were not—we had no such luxuries even at Danforth's—and the illustrious Gayetey and his compeers had not yet replaced the newspaper with their tissues. The light was from candles and whale oil lamps that it always was a bore to get started. The water of the Back Bay came up to Arlington Street and the Public Garden was a dreary waste. You got from Cambridge by omnibus—and might return part way by rail from the Fitchburg station and then by horse car (not street car) to the neighborhood of the Law School Building. This was all before the war, when I was a boy. Some things that happened after it would seem rather ancient history to most of you. It would seem remote to the lawyers when I say that I have sat on the Bench with Lord Chancellor Cranworth and have dined with Baron Parke. It will have a meaning to everyone when I say that I have talked with a schoolmate of Byron's and a friend of Charles Lamb's—Barry Cornwall. The war itself, though it started the changes that almost have made a new art of warfare—such as the field telegraph, breech loaders, and ironclads

—sounds nowadays pretty remote in its methods. We fought in two close ranks, the rear rank firing over the shoulders of the front. A regiment would be wiped out if it tried it now. Yet I remember seeing what I suppose was the germ of that which made it impossible, in the shape of a little go-cart with a gunbarrel on top that it was said would grind out a stream of bullets like a hose, on the Peninsula, at Malvern Hill. I never heard that it succeeded and at the time I supposed that it stood on the plane of Christian Commission Crackers that I also saw, with Come to Jesus printed on their side.

But after all our interests are in the present and the future—not in the past. They are our real topics and for any man who is not superannuated the question is what he has to say about them. I have learned to distrust the melodramatic completeness of simple formulas and do not put much faith in prophecy. Twenty years ago I was much stirred by Pearson's prediction that by mere spread of population in the torrid and middle zone the yellow race would come out ahead of us in the long run and that we should be put on the defensive. And to this day I am by that of James J. Hill as to the exhaustion of our resources. But Pearson's denouement is too far ahead and I console myself even when I think of Mr. Hill's. If he is right we shall support a smaller population than otherwise and there may be less scope for abilities like his which seem to me one of the greatest types of human power. But little peoples and small populations have done things in their day and may again. Athens could not have kept New York going for ten days, I suppose, but it counts for more than the United States. Perhaps in the future we shall care less for quantity and more for quality and try to breed a race. There would be compensations even if we had to drop from James Hill to Aeschylus and Aristotle. Perhaps by the self-defeat of nature to which Hegel called attention civilization will cut its own throat, or as Flinders Petrie thinks there may [be] discoverable cycles of its rise, decline, and fall. But even then we hope that some survivors will pass on the torch as the two men of '60 passed on the vital current of this Club. Whatever else we learn from nature we learn from it a mystic faith.

I have been reading lately a golden book, or rather books, for there are ten volumes of it: Fabre's *Souvenirs Entomologiques*. It is a seed book. There I am very sure is the source of that echo from behind phenomena that for a moment we think we hear in Maeterlinck's *Bees*. I think it must have inspired one of the most noticeable traits in Bergson's philosophy. It is simply the exquisitely told tale of a life-long watch of beetles and wasps, but from it we learn the faith I spoke of if we had it not before. I heard the doctrine years ago from Dr. Bartol. He spoke of the hen hatching her eggs in obedience to a destiny she did not understand. Fabre tells us of grubs born and having passed their whole lives in the heart of an oak that when, after three years, the time for metamorphosis comes, build a chamber that as grubs they do not need with a broad passage for the beetle that is to be. They obey their destiny without any sight of the promised land. The law of the grub and the hen is the law also for man. We all have cosmic destinies of which we cannot divine the end, if the unknown has ends. Our business is to commit ourselves to life, to accept at once our functions and our ignorance and to offer our heart to fate. When one is drawing near the end it is a great happiness to be assured for a moment by friends such as I see around me that one has borne one's part and has not failed in the faith.

LAW AND THE COURT

Speech at a Dinner of the Harvard Law School Association of New York on February 15, 1913

MR. CHAIRMAN AND GENTLEMEN: Vanity is the most philosophical of those feelings that we are taught to despise. For vanity recognizes that if a man is in a minority of one we lock him up, and therefore longs for an assurance from others that one's work has not been in vain. If a man's ambition is the thirst for a power that comes not from office but from within, he never can be sure that any happiness is not a fool's paradise—he never can be sure that he sits on that other bench reserved for the masters of those who know. Then too, at least until one draws near to seventy, one is less likely to hear the trumpets than the rolling fire of the front. I have passed that age, but I still am on the firing line, and it is only in rare moments like this that there comes a pause and for half an hour one feels a trembling hope. They are the rewards of a lifetime's work.

But let me turn to more palpable realities—to that other visible Court to which for ten now accomplished years it has been my opportunity to belong. We are very quiet there, but it is the quiet of a storm center, as we all know. Science has taught the world skepticism and has made it legitimate to put everything to the test of proof. Many beautiful and noble reverences are impaired, but in these days no one can complain if any institution, system, or belief is called on to justify its continuance in life. Of course we are not excepted and have not escaped. Doubts are expressed that go to our very being. Not only are we told that when Marshall pronounced an Act of Congress unconstitutional he usurped a power that the Constitution did not give, but we are told that we are the representatives of a class—a tool of the money power. I get letters, not always anonymous, intimating that we are corrupt. Well, gentlemen, I admit that it makes my heart ache. It is very painful, when one spends all the energies of one's soul in trying to do good work, with no thought but that of solving a problem according to the rules by which one is bound, to know that many see sinister motives and would be glad of evidence that one was consciously bad. But we must take such things philosophically and try to see what we can learn from hatred and distrust and whether behind them there may not be some germ of inarticulate truth.

The attacks upon the Court are merely an expression of the unrest that seems to wonder vaguely whether law and order pay. When the ignorant are taught to doubt they do not know what they safely may believe. And it seems to me that at this time we need education in the obvious more than investigation of the obscure. I do not see so much immediate use in committees on the high cost of living and inquiries how far it is due to the increased production of gold, how far to the narrowing of cattle ranges and the growth of population, how far to the bugaboo, as I do in bringing home to people a few social and economic truths. Most men think dramatically, not quantitatively, a fact that the rich would be wise to remember more than they do. We are apt to contrast the palace with the hovel, the dinner at Sherry's with the working man's pail, and never ask how much or realize how little is withdrawn to make the prizes of success (subordinate prizes—since the only prize much cared for by the powerful is power. The prize of the general is not a bigger tent, but command.). We are apt to think of ownership as a terminus, not as a gateway, and not to realize that except the tax levied for personal consumption large ownership means investment, and investment means the direction of labor towards the production of the greatest returns—returns that so far as they are great show by that very fact that they are consumed by the many, not alone by the few. If I may ride a hobby for an instant, I should say we need to think things instead of words—to drop ownership, money, etc., and to think of the stream of products; of wheat and cloth and railway travel. When we do it is obvious that the many consume them; that they now as truly have substantially all there is, as if the title were in the United States; that the great body of property is socially administered now, and that the function of private ownership is to divine in advance the equilibrium of social desires—which socialism equally would have to divine, but which, under the illusion of self-seeking, is more poignantly and shrewdly foreseen.

I should like to see it brought home to the public that the question of fair prices is due to the fact that none of us can have as much as we want of all the things we want; that as less will be produced than the public wants, the question is how much of each product it will have and how much go without; that thus the final competition is between the objects of desire, and therefore between the producers of those objects; that when we oppose labor and capital, labor means the group that is selling its product and capital all the other groups that are buying it. The hated capitalist is simply the mediator, the prophet, the adjuster according to his divination of the future desire. If you could get that believed, the body of the people would have no doubt as to the worth of law.

That is my outside thought on the present discontents. As to the truth embodied in them, in part it cannot be helped. It cannot be helped, it is as it should be, that the law is behind the times. I told a labor leader once that what they asked was favor, and if a decision was against them they called it wicked. The same might be said of their opponents. It means that the law is growing. As law embodies beliefs that have triumphed in the battle of ideas and then have translated themselves into action, while there still is doubt, while opposite convictions still keep a battle front against each other, the time for law has not come; the notion destined to prevail is not yet entitled to the field. It is a misfortune if a judge reads his conscious or unconscious sympathy with one side or the other prematurely into the law, and forgets that what seem to him to be first principles are believed by half his fellow men to be wrong. I think that we have suffered from this misfortune, in State courts at least, and that this is another and very important truth to be extracted from the popular discontent. When twenty years ago a vague terror went over the earth and the word socialism began to be heard, I thought and still think that fear was translated into doctrines that had no proper place in the Constitution or the common law. Judges are apt to be naif, simple-minded men, and they need something of Mephistopheles. We too need education in the obvious—to learn to transcend our own convictions and to leave room for much that we hold dear to be done away with short of revolution by the orderly change of law.

I have no belief in panaceas and almost none in sudden ruin. I believe with Montesquieu that if the chance of a battle—I may add, the passage of a law—has ruined a state, there was a general cause at work that made the state ready to perish by a single battle or law. Hence I am not much interested one way or the other in the nostrums now so strenuously urged. I do not think the United States would come to an end if we lost our power to declare an Act of Congress void. I do think the Union would be imperiled if we could not make that declaration as to the laws of the several States. For one in my place sees how often a local policy prevails with those who are not trained to national views and how often action is taken that embodies what the Commerce Clause was meant to end. But I am not aware that there is any serious desire to limit the Court's power in this regard. For most of the things that properly can be called evils in the present state of law I think the main remedy, as for the evils of public opinion, is for us to grow more civilized.

If I am right it will be a slow business for our people to reach rational views, assuming that we are allowed to work peaceably to that end. But as I grow older I grow calm. If I feel what are perhaps an old man's apprehensions, that competition from new races will cut deeper than working men's disputes and will test whether we can hang together and can fight; if I fear that we are running through the world's resources at a pace that we cannot keep; I do not lose my hopes. I do not pin my dreams for the future to my country or even to my race. I think it probable that civilization somehow will last as long as I care to look ahead—perhaps with smaller numbers, but perhaps also bred to greatness and splendor by science. I think it not improbable that man, like the grub that prepares a chamber for the winged thing it never has seen but is to be—that man may have cosmic destinies that he does not understand. And so beyond the vision of battling races and an impoverished earth I catch a dreaming glimpse of peace.

The other day my dream was pictured to my mind. It was evening. I was walking homeward on Pennsylvania Avenue near the Treasury, and as I looked beyond Sherman's Statue to the west the sky was aflame with scarlet and crimson from the setting sun. But, like the note of downfall in Wagner's opera, below the sky line there came from little globes the pallid discord of the electric lights. And I thought to myself the Götterdämmerung will end, and from those globes clustered like evil eggs will come the new masters of the sky. It is like the time in which we live. But then I remembered the faith that I partly have expressed, faith in a universe not measured by our fears, a universe that has thought and more than thought inside of it, and as I gazed, after the sunset and above the electric lights there shone the stars.

TRIBUTE TO JOHN CHIPMAN GRAY

Read at the Massachusetts Historical Society, March 12, 1915

THE AFFECTIONATE intimacy of a lifetime may not be the best preparation for an attempt to characterize a friend whom one has known and loved so long. His qualities come to be felt too instinctively for articulate enumeration just as one ceases to be conscious of the judgments that govern one's walk in the streets. But with so marked a personality as that of John Gray, there were features that no one could forget.

He came of a family in which scholarship was in the blood; and I think that perhaps the first thought that would occur to me would be that he was a scholar born. He was a scholar of a type that is growing rare. For his knowledge, his immense reading, his memory were not confined to the actualities of the day. Alongside of mathematics, and the latest German works on jurisprudence, alongside of his mastery of the law, equally profound and available for teaching in the Law School and advising upon great affairs, he not only kept up the study of Greek and Roman classics, but he was familiar

SOURCE: *Proceedings, Massachusetts Historical Society*, XLVIII, 323 (1915).

with a thousand bypaths among books. I think he could have given a clear account of the Bangorian controversy, the very name of which has been forgotten by most of us, and he could have recited upon all manner of curious memoirs or upon pretty much any theme that falls within the domain of literature, properly so called. He loved books, and his beautiful collection ranged from the Theodosian code to curious eighteenth century tracts.

He brought this scholarship to bear unobtrusively but powerfully when he came to write. His treatises on *Perpetuities* is a quiet masterpiece that stands on an equal footing with the most famous works of the great English writers upon property law. His last little book on *The Nature and Sources of the Law* is worthy of the German professors who might seem to have made that theme their private domain. But unlike much German work, instead of pedantry, it is written with the light touch and humor of a man of the world. For his knowledge not only was converted into the organic tissue of wisdom, but flowered with a quiet humor that sometimes emerged in his writing and that gave habitual delightfulness to his talk.

He was a very wise man. So wise that those who met him in affairs perhaps would say that wisdom was the first thing to be mentioned with his name. He was able as no one else has been to unite practice in Boston, in which he was consulted and relied upon in matters of the largest import, with teaching at the Law School, where his subjects required study of subjects that seemed most remote from every day; and both with equal success.

In this connection, it is worth recalling that when he was in the army he was the first officer to meet Sherman at Savannah after the march to the sea, and that he is referred to in Sherman's report of his operations as "a very intelligent officer whose name I have forgotten," a striking tribute to one who barely had reached manhood from the great commander at the crowning moment of his success.

Such capacity as Gray's for voluminous occupation is apt to go with a loose fiber, or, one might say, a somewhat coarse grain, but Gray was delicate, accurate, and fine grained. Like all his race, he was keenly observing without showing it, seeming to see from the sides of his eyes like a woman. And none of his remarkable qualities and capacities remained isolated or futile, but they all united to give character to the stream of his thought. It will be seen that I am trying to describe a master, one who fairly may be called a great master, who was listened to with equal respect by clients, by courts, and by all students of the law, and at the same time an extraordinary and delightful man, whose conversation gave equal pleasure to specialists and men of the world. When I add to this that he was a most faithful and affectionate friend, I have said enough perhaps to show, I will not say what a loss is his death, for he had lived as long as a man can hope to live, but what a gain, not only to us who loved him, but to the world, was his life, a life rich in fruits and ending surrounded by honor and by love.

THE RACE IS OVER

Radio Address to the Nation,
March 8, 1931

In this symposium my part is only to sit in silence. To express one's feelings as the end draws near is too intimate a task. But I may mention one thought that comes to me as a listener-in. The riders in a race do not stop short when they reach the goal. There is a little finishing canter before coming to a standstill. There is time to hear the kind voice of friends and to say to one's self: "The work is done." But just as one says that, the answer comes: "The race is over, but the work never is done while the power to work remains." The canter that brings you to a standstill need not be only coming to rest. It cannot be, while you still live. For to live is to function. That is all there is in living.

And so I end with a line from a Latin poet who uttered the message more than fifteen hundred years ago:

"Death plucks my ear and says, 'Live—I am coming.' "

Source: a manuscript copy, in Holmes's hand, preserved among the Holmes papers at the Harvard Law School. The original is shown on the facing page.

In this symposium my part is only to sit in silence. To express one's feelings as the end draws near is too intimate a task. But I may mention one thought that comes to me as a listener in. The riders in a race do not stop short when they reach the goal. There is a little finishing canter before coming to a standstill. There is time to hear the kind voice of friends and to say to oneself: "The work is done." But just as one says that, the answer comes: "The race is over, but the work never is done while the power to work remains." The canter that brings you to a standstill need not be only coming to rest. It cannot be, while you still live. For to live is to function. That is all there is in living. And so I end with a line from a Latin poet who uttered the message more than fifteen hundred years ago, "Death plucks my ear and says 'Live—I am coming.'"

Bei Fragen zur Produktsicherheit wenden Sie sich bitte an:
If you have any questions regarding product safety,
please contact:

Walter de Gruyter GmbH
Genthiner Straße 13
10785 Berlin
productsafety@degruyterbrill.com